Jesus

PUBLISHING

Torrance, California

© 2009 Bristol Works, Inc.
Rose Publishing, Inc.
4733 Torrance Blvd., #259
Torrance, California 90503 U.S.A.
Email: info@rose-publishing.com
www.rose-publishing.com

Includes these Rose Publishing Titles:

Who is Jesus? ©2009 Bristol Works, Inc.
Jesus: Fact & Fiction ©2008 Bristol Works, Inc.
        Principal Author: Robert M. Bowman, Jr., MA
        General Editor: Paul Carden
Gospels Side by Side ©2008 Bristol Works, Inc.
        Contributing Authors: Willam Brent Ashby, BT; Benjamin Galan, MTS, ThM
The Beatitudes ©2008 Bristol Works, Inc.
        Contributing Authors: Willam Brent Ashby, BT; Benjamin Galan, MTS, ThM
The Lord's Prayer ©2007 Bristol Works, Inc.
Names of Jesus ©2006 RW Research, Inc.
        Author: William Brent Ashby, BT
Christ in the Old Testament ©2007 Bristol Works, Inc.
        Contributing Authors: Willam Brent Ashby, BT; Benjamin Galan, MTS, ThM
Christ in the Passover ©2008 Bristol Works, Inc.
        Author: Benjamin Galan, MTS, ThM
        Consultant: Rev. Barry Goldman

Many of these titles are available as individual pamphlets, as wall charts, and as ready-to-use PowerPoint® presentations.

Library of Congress Cataloging-in-Publication Data

Jesus.
        p. cm. – (Rose Bible basics)
    ISBN 978-1-59636-324-3 (pbk.)
    1. Jesus Christ–Person and offices–Biblical teaching.
    BT203.J469 2009
    232–dc22
                                        2008055615

Printed by Regent Publishing Services Ltd.
Printed in China
February 2012, Third printing

JESUS

Contents

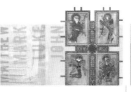

Continued
on next
page

→

JESUS

Contents

Who is Jesus?

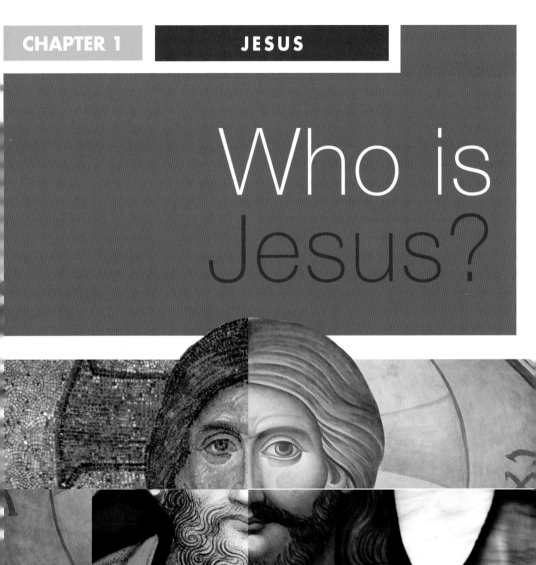

Why Did He Come?

What Did He Say?

Why Did He Die?

"Who do people say the Son of Man is?"
—Matthew 16:13

Jesus asked this question about himself to his disciples around 2,000 years ago. His disciples replied with answers based on things they knew or had experienced: "Some say John the Baptist; others say Elijah; and still others, Jeremiah or one of the prophets" (v. 14).

People in Jesus' day had expectations about who he was and arrived at their conclusions based on those expectations. Today it is not very different. People gather ideas about Jesus from many places: from television and movies, from books and newspapers, from family, school, and office conversations. Some of these ideas are right on the mark—others miss the mark entirely.

Some people say Jesus was just a popular preacher or a guru of ethical living. Others say it is not even important to know who Jesus is. But for people who have given their lives to Jesus and have experienced life in a new and wonderful way, the question about Jesus' identity is of greater-than-life importance.

After asking his disciples what other people say about him, Jesus turned to them and asked, "But what about you? Who do you say I am?" (v. 15). Peter answered, "You are the Christ, the Son of the living God" (v. 16).

What does it mean that Jesus is "the Christ" and "the Son"? It means that he is much more than a popular preacher, a prophet, or a wise teacher. Who is Jesus? The following pages will answer this fundamental question. To understand who Jesus is, it is important to understand what he taught, how he lived, what he claimed about himself, and what those who knew him best said—those who knew him as "the Christ, the Son of the living God."

1. Who is Jesus?

What Jesus said

"I am the way and the truth and the life. No one comes to the Father except through me."—John 14:6

"I am the bread of life. He who comes to me will never go hungry, and he who believes in me will never be thirsty.... And this is the will of him who sent me, that I shall lose none of all that he has given me, but raise them up at the last day. For my Father's will is that everyone who looks to the Son and believes in him shall have eternal life, and I will raise him up at the last day."—John 6:35–40

"I am the light of the world. Whoever follows me will never walk in darkness, but will have the light of life.'"—John 8:12

See also Matthew 11:27–29; John 8:58; 10:30.

What those who knew him best said

"In the beginning was the Word, and the Word was with God, and the Word was God. He was with God in the beginning. Through him all things were made; without him nothing was made that has been made. In him was life, and that life was the light of men.... The Word became flesh and made his dwelling among us. We have seen his glory, the glory of the One and Only, who came from the Father, full of grace and truth.... From the fullness of his grace we have all received one blessing after another. For the law was given through Moses; grace and truth came through Jesus Christ."—John 1:1–4, 14–17

John was one of Jesus' closest friends and earliest followers who was at the scene of Jesus' execution.

"For you know that it was not with perishable things such as silver or gold that you were redeemed from the empty way of life handed down to you from your forefathers, but with the precious blood of Christ, a lamb without blemish or defect. He was chosen before the creation of the world, but was revealed in these last times for your sake."—1 Peter 1:18–20

Peter, one of Jesus' twelve disciples, wrote this to Christians in the first century AD.

See also Matthew 16:16; Colossians 2:9; Hebrews 1:3.

What God the Father said

"While [Peter] was still speaking, a bright cloud enveloped them, and a voice from the cloud said, 'This is my Son, whom I love; with him I am well pleased. Listen to him!'"—Matthew 17:5

God the Father spoke plainly about Jesus.

What nature said

"Jesus was in the stern, sleeping on a cushion. The disciples woke him and said to him, 'Teacher, don't you care if we drown?' He got up, rebuked the wind and said to the waves, 'Quiet! Be still!' Then the wind died down and it was completely calm. He said to his disciples, 'Why are you so afraid? Do you still have no faith?' They were terrified and asked each other, 'Who is this? Even the wind and the waves obey him!'"—Mark 4:38–41

The natural world obeyed Jesus' commands because he is its Creator.

See also Matthew 14:13–33.

What the demons said

"In the synagogue there was a man possessed by a demon, an evil spirit. He cried out at the top of his voice, 'Ha! What do you want with us, Jesus of Nazareth? Have you come to destroy us? I know who you are—the Holy One of God!'"—Luke 4:33–34

The spiritual world recognized Jesus and his power.

See also Matthew 8:29; Mark 5:6–7.

Christ in The Storm on The Sea of Galilee
by Rembrandt

What others have said

"We may note in passing that He was never regarded as a mere moral teacher. He did not produce that effect on any of the people who actually met Him. He produced mainly three effects—Hatred—Terror—Adoration. There was no trace of people expressing mild approval."—C.S. Lewis, Oxford and Cambridge professor and former agnostic (1898–1963)

"I know men and I tell you that Jesus Christ is no mere man. Between him and every other person in the world there is no possible term of comparison."
—Napoleon Bonaparte, French Emperor (1769–1821)

"Why don't the names of Buddha, Mohammed, Confucius offend people? The reason is that these others didn't claim to be God, but Jesus did."—Josh McDowell, Christian Evangelist

"He possessed neither wealth nor influence. His relatives were inconspicuous, and had neither training nor formal education. In infancy He startled a king; in childhood He puzzled doctors; in manhood He ruled the course of nature, walked upon the billows as if pavement, and hushed the sea to sleep. He healed the multitudes without medicine and made no charge for His service. The names of the past proud statesmen of Greece and Rome have come and gone. The names of the past scientists, philosophers, and theologians have come and gone; but the name of this Man abounds more and more. Though time has spread nineteen hundred years between the people of this generation and the scene of His crucifixion, yet He still lives, Herod could not destroy Him, and the grave could not hold Him."—from "The Incomparable Christ"

Summary: Jesus was more than human. In fact, he was human and divine at the same time—the Son of God. He is the Creator who entered his creation.

2. What was his message?

What Jesus said about his good news (gospel)

"The time has come.... The kingdom of God is near. Repent and believe the good news!"—Mark 1:15

"And this is the will of him who sent me, that I shall lose none of all that he has given me, but raise them up at the last day. For my Father's will is that everyone who looks to the Son and believes in him shall have eternal life, and I will raise him up at the last day."—John 6:39–40

See also Matthew 4:23–24, 5:1–7:29; Mark 4:1–34; Luke 15:1–31; John 10:1–18; 15:1–17.

What those who knew him best said

"We are witnesses of everything he did in the country of the Jews and in Jerusalem. They killed him by hanging him on a tree, but God raised him from the dead on the third day and caused him to be seen. He was not seen by all the people, but by witnesses whom God had already chosen—by us who ate and drank with him after he rose from the dead. He commanded us to preach to the people and to testify that he is the one whom God appointed as judge of the living and the dead. All the prophets testify about him that everyone who believes in him receives forgiveness of sins through his name."—Acts 10:39–43

Spoken by Peter, one of Jesus' best friends, who was hand-picked by Jesus to be a leader after Jesus' death and resurrection.

See also Acts 2:14–41; 3:11–26; 4:8–12; 5:29–32.

What others have said

"The real truth is that while He came to preach the gospel, His chief object in coming was that there might be a gospel to preach."—R.W. Dale, Congregationalist minister (1829–1895)

"Jesus does not give recipes that show the way to God as other teachers of religion do, He is himself the way."—Karl Barth, Theologian (1886–1968)

"The Gospel that represents Jesus Christ, not as a system of truth to be received, into the mind, as I should receive a system of philosophy, or astronomy, but it represents Him as a real, living, mighty Savior, able to save me now."—Catherine Booth, Cofounder of the Salvation Army (1829–1890)

Summary: The center of Jesus' message was himself. He impacted the world like no other human in history. Everything he did was good, and the greatest good he accomplished was through his death and rising from the dead. The good news he came to announce was also what he came to accomplish.

What Jesus said about:

Love

"Love the Lord your God with all your heart and with all your soul and with all your mind and with all your strength. Love your neighbor as yourself. There is no commandment greater than these."—Mark 12:30–31

"Do to others as you would have them do to you. If you love those who love you, what credit is that to you? Even sinners love those who love them. And if you do good to those who are good to you, what credit is that to you? Even sinners do that…. But love your enemies, do good to them, and lend to them without expecting to get anything back. Then your reward will be great, and you will be sons of the Most High, because he is kind to the ungrateful and wicked. Be merciful, just as your Father is merciful."—Luke 6:31–36

"A new command I give you: Love one another. As I have loved you, so you must love one another. By this all men will know that you are my disciples, if you love one another."—John 13:34–35

"Whoever has my commands and obeys them, he is the one who loves me. He who loves me will be loved by my Father, and I too will love him and show myself to him."—John 14:21

God

"No one is good—except God alone."—Mark 10:18

"You are the ones who justify yourselves in the eyes of men, but God knows your hearts. What is highly valued among men is detestable in God's sight."—Luke 16:15

"[The disciples] were greatly astonished and asked, 'Who then can be saved?' Jesus looked at them and said, 'With man this is impossible, but with God all things are possible.'"—Matthew 19:25–26

"God is spirit, and his worshipers must worship in spirit and in truth."—John 4:24

Heaven

"Store up for yourselves treasures in heaven, where moth and rust do not destroy, and where thieves do not break in and steal. For where your treasure is, there your heart will be also."—Matthew 6:20–21

"There will be more rejoicing in heaven over one sinner who repents than over ninety-nine righteous persons who do not need to repent."—Luke 15:7

"Do not let your hearts be troubled. Trust in God; trust also in me. In my Father's house are many rooms. I am going there to prepare a place for you. And if I go and prepare a place for you, I will come back and take you to be with me that you also may be where I am."—John 14:1–4

3. Why did he come?

What Jesus said

"For God did not send his Son into the world to condemn the world, but to save the world through him."—John 3:17

"I tell you the truth, I am the gate for the sheep. All who ever came before me were thieves and robbers, but the sheep did not listen to them. I am the gate; whoever enters through me will be saved.... I have come that they may have life, and have it to the full."—John 10:7–10

See also Matthew 5:17; Mark 2:17; 10:45; Luke 12:49–51; 19:10; John 7:28; 9:39; 12:46.

What those who knew him best said

"Christ Jesus came into the world to save sinners—of whom I am the worst."
—1 Timothy 1:15

Written by the Apostle Paul who was viciously anti-Christian until a life-changing encounter with the resurrected Jesus.

See also John 1:11–12; 1 John 3:8.

What the prophets said

"Surely he took up our infirmities and carried our sorrows, yet we considered him stricken by God, smitten by him, and afflicted."—Isaiah 53:4

Spoken by Isaiah, a prophet who saw what the Messiah (the Christ) would do more than 700 years before Jesus was born.

See also Genesis 49:10; Malachi 3:1–4.

What others have said

"The essence of Jesus' ministry was to bring the divine power into all the realms of death and thereby to call into question the finality of death. Light in the darkness, the mocker of the grave, divine love in the most godforsaken places, Jesus throws off balance the whole world of the small soul."
—Robert Barron, Professor of Systematic Theology, Mundelein Seminary

"Nineteen centuries have come and gone and today he is the centerpiece of the human race and the leader of the column of progress. I am far within the mark when I say that all the armies that ever marched, all the navies that ever were built; all the parliaments that ever sat and all the kings that ever reigned, put together, have not affected the life of man upon this earth as powerfully as has that one solitary life."—Attributed to James Allen Francis, Doctor of Divinity (1864–1928)

Summary: Jesus came to save the world.

4. Why did he die?

What Jesus said

"From that time on Jesus began to explain to his disciples that he must go to Jerusalem and suffer many things at the hands of the elders, chief priests and teachers of the law, and that he must be killed and on the third day be raised to life."—Matthew 16:21

"He said to them, 'How foolish you are, and how slow of heart to believe all that the prophets have spoken! Did not the Christ have to suffer these things and then enter his glory?' And beginning with Moses and all the Prophets, he explained to them what was said in all the Scriptures concerning himself."
—Luke 24:25–27

See also Matthew 26:26–29; Mark 9:30–31; 10:32–34, 45; Luke 18:31–33; John 3:14–15; 8:28; 12:32–33.

The Flagellation of Our Lord Jesus Christ by William A. Bouguereau

What the first Christians said

"But now a righteousness from God, apart from law, has been made known, to which the Law and the Prophets testify. This righteousness from God comes through faith in Jesus Christ to all who believe. There is no difference, for all have sinned and fall short of the glory of God, and are justified freely by his grace through the redemption that came by Christ Jesus. God presented him as a sacrifice of atonement, through faith in his blood. He did this to demonstrate his justice, because in his forbearance he had left the sins committed beforehand unpunished—he did it to demonstrate his justice at the present time, so as to be just and the one who justifies those who have faith in Jesus."
—Romans 3:21–26

Paul wrote this to Christians in Rome, approximately AD 56.

See also Acts 2:22–41; 3:13–20; 1Timothy 2:5–6; Titus 2:13–14; Hebrews 9:28; 1 Peter 1:18–20.

What the prophets said

"And I will pour out on the house of David and the inhabitants of Jerusalem a spirit of grace and supplication. They will look on me, the one they have pierced, and they will mourn for him as one mourns for an only child.... On that day a fountain will be opened to the house of David and the inhabitants of

Jerusalem, to cleanse them from sin and impurity."—Zechariah 12:10, 13:1
Spoken by the prophet Zechariah, approximately 400 years before Jesus, foretelling what would happen to the Messiah, the Christ.

See also Isaiah 52:13–53:12; Daniel 9:26; Psalm 22.

What others have said

"If Jesus Christ was who He claimed to be, and He did die on a Cross at a point of time in history, then, for all history past and all history future it is relevant because that is the very focal point for forgiveness and redemption."
—Josh McDowell

"They nailed Him to a tree, not knowing that by that very act they were bringing the world to His feet. They gave Him a cross, not guessing that He would make it a throne. They flung Him outside the gates to die, not knowing that in that very moment they were lifting up all the gates of the universe, to let the King come in. They thought to root out His doctrines, not understanding that they were implanting imperishably in the hearts of men the very name they intended to destroy. They thought they had God with His back to the wall, pinned and helpless and defeated; they did not know that it was God Himself who had tracked them down. He did not conquer in spite of the dark mystery of evil. He conquered through it."—James S. Stewart, Presbyterian preacher (1896–1990)

"It was not for societies or states, that Christ died, but for men."—C.S. Lewis

"No man ever loved like Jesus. He taught the blind to see and the dumb to speak. He died on the cross to save us. He bore our sins. And now God says, 'Because He did, I can forgive you.'"—Billy Graham

Christ Healing The Blind Man by El Greco

Summary: The Messiah's death was predicted long before he walked the earth. As the Messiah (the Christ), Jesus willingly allowed himself be put to death on the cross. In this way, he was sacrificed for the sins of all people. By dying a criminal's death through a miscarriage of human justice, Jesus balanced the scales of God's justice for the debt owed by the human race. Because of this, all who trust in him can be forgiven and receive salvation.

5. What about the empty tomb?

What Jesus said

"[Jesus] said to them, 'This is what I told you while I was still with you: Everything must be fulfilled that is written about me in the Law of Moses, the Prophets and the Psalms.' Then he opened their minds so they could understand the Scriptures. He told them, 'This is what is written: The Christ will suffer and rise from the dead on the third day, and repentance and forgiveness of sins will be preached in his name to all nations, beginning at Jerusalem. You are witnesses of these things.'"—Luke 24:44–48

"A week later [after the empty tomb was discovered] his disciples were in the house again, and Thomas was with them. Though the doors were locked, Jesus came and stood among them and said, 'Peace be with you!' Then he said to Thomas, 'Put your finger here; see my hands. Reach out your hand and put it into my side. Stop doubting and believe.' Thomas said to him, 'My Lord and my God!'"—John 20:26–28

What the messengers at Jesus' empty tomb said

"On the first day of the week, very early in the morning, the women took spices they had prepared and went to the tomb. They found the stone rolled away from the tomb but when they entered, they did not find the body of the Lord Jesus. While they were wondering about this, suddenly two men in clothes that gleamed like lightening stood beside them. In their fright the women bowed down with their faces to the ground, but the men said to them, 'Why do you look for the living among the dead? He is not here; he has risen!'"—Luke 24:1–6

The Resurrection by Carl Heinrich Bloch

Like these the first messengers, the first Christians went on to boldly proclaim that Jesus had risen!

What the first Christians said

"For what I received I passed on to you as of first importance: that Christ died for our sins according to the Scriptures, that he was buried, that he was raised on the third day according to the Scriptures, and that he appeared to Peter, and then to the Twelve. After that, he appeared to more than five hundred of the brothers at the same time."—1 Corinthians 15:3–6

This was the testimony that the Apostle Paul passed on to believers.

See also Matthew 28; Mark 16; John 20, 21; Acts 1:1–11; 2:22–36; 3:15–22; 1 Corinthians 15:3–8; Colossians 3:1; 1 Peter 3:18–22.

What others have said

"The Resurrection is the central theme in every Christian sermon reported in the Acts. The Resurrection, and its consequences were the 'gospel' or good news which the Christians brought."—C.S. Lewis

"Now there was about this time Jesus, a wise man, if it be lawful to call him a man; for he was a doer of wonderful works, a teacher of such men as receive the truth with pleasure. He drew over to him many Jews, and also many of the Greeks. This man was the Christ. And when Pilate had condemned him to the cross, upon his impeachment by the principal men among us, those who had loved him from the first did not forsake him, for he appeared to them alive on the third day, the divine prophets having spoken these and thousands of other wonderful things about him."—Josephus, Jewish historian (c. AD 37–100)

"[The Resurrection] is truly of great importance in Christianity; so great that His being or not being the Messiah stands or falls with it: so that these two important articles are inseparable and in effect make one. For since that time, believe one and you believe both; deny one of them, and you can believe neither."—John Locke, English philosopher (1632–1704)

"Confucius' tomb   –   occupied
Buddha's tomb   –   occupied
Mohammed's tomb –   occupied
Jesus' tomb   –   EMPTY."
—G.B. Hardy, Canadian scientist

Summary: There is no other adequate explanation for the empty tomb and the subsequent events than that Jesus rose up alive from the grave and was seen by many people, and that many of those same people saw him rise up into heaven.

© Tiffany Chan

Life of Jesus

Dating assumes Jesus was born approximately 4 BC
All dates are approximate.

4 BC

Jesus is born in Bethlehem Luke 2:1–7
Jesus is presented in the temple Luke 2:21–38
Mary and Joseph flee with their child Jesus to Egypt to escape
    King Herod's persecution Matthew 2:13–18
The family returns to the hometown of Nazareth Matthew 2:19–21
Jesus grows up in Nazareth Matthew 2:22–23
At age 12, Jesus amazes teachers of the Jewish law Luke 2:41–50

AD 27

Jesus is baptized by John the Baptist Matthew 3:13–17
Jesus is tempted by Satan but does not sin Matthew 4:1–11
Jesus' first disciples John 1:38–51
Jesus' first miracle: water changed to wine John 2:6–10
Jesus in Jerusalem for the annual Passover celebration John 2:13
Jesus cleanses the temple of sellers who had made the holy place into
    a market John 2:14–16
At Cana, Jesus heals a royal official's son John 4:46–53
Jesus ministers in Galilee Matthew 4:13–17

AD 28

Jesus reads from Isaiah and is rejected Luke 4:14–30
Jesus heals people with various diseases and those possessed by demons
    Luke 4:31–41
Jesus heals and forgives the sins of a paralyzed man Luke 5:17–26
Jesus in Jerusalem for Passover John 5:1
Jesus heals a crippled man at the Pool of Bethesda in Jerusalem John 5:2–9
Jesus calls the tax-collector, Levi (Matthew), to be his follower Luke 5:27–32
The Sermon on the Mount and the Beatitudes Matthew 5:1–7:29
Jesus heals a centurion's servant Matthew 8:5–13
Jesus raises a widow's son from the dead Luke 7:12–15
Jesus calms a storm Luke 8:22–25
Jesus heals Jairus's daughter and woman with hemorrhage Mark 5:21–43
Jesus heals a blind man Matthew 9:27–34

AD 29

Jesus sends out the 12 apostles to heal diseases and drive out evil spirits
    Matthew 10:1–42
Jesus is accused of being out of his mind and using Satan's power
    Mark 3:19–27
King Herod beheads John the Baptist Matthew 14:3–12
The 12 apostles return Luke 9:10
Jesus miraculously feeds 5,000 people with five loaves of bread and
    two fish Mark 6:38–44

Jesus walks on water Matthew 14:25
Jesus in Jerusalem for Passover John 6:4
Jesus heals a deaf man who cannot speak Mark 7:32–37
Jesus restores sight to a blind man Mark 8:22–26
Peter declares that Jesus is the Son of God Matthew 16:13–20
Jesus predicts his death Matthew 16:21–28
The Transfiguration Luke 9:29–36
Jesus heals a boy with an evil spirit Mark 9:17–27
Jesus again predicts his death Matthew 17:22–23
Jesus sends out 72 disciples Luke 10:1–16
Jesus forgives a woman caught in adultery John 7:53–8:11
Healing a man born blind John 9:1–41

Jesus heals a crippled woman Luke 13:11–13
Jesus raises Lazarus from the dead John 11:1–46
Jesus heals 10 men with leprosy, but only one returns to give thanks
    Luke 17:11–19
Jesus predicts his death for a third time Matthew 20:17–19
Jesus heals blind Bartimaeus Mark 10:46–52
Jesus stays with Zacchaeus, a wealthy and repentant man Luke 19:1–10
Mary anoints the feet of Jesus John 12:1–9

Palm Sunday and the week following
Palm Sunday: Jesus triumphantly enters Jerusalem
Monday: Jesus clears the temple
Tuesday: Jesus teaches in parables
Wednesday: Jesus rests
Thursday: Jesus celebrates Passover, the Last Supper, and is betrayed
    by his disciple Judas
Friday: Jesus is arrested by Roman authorities, crucified on the cross,
    and buried in a tomb
Friday afternoon, Saturday, Sunday morning: Jesus in the tomb
Sunday: Jesus' resurrection

Appearance of the Risen Christ
Jesus' tomb found empty by the women Luke 24:1–8
Jesus appears to Mary Magdalene John 20:11–18
Jesus appears on the road to Emmaus Luke 24:13–35
Jesus appears to ten of his disciples John 20:19–24
Thomas doubts but is convinced when he sees and touches the
    risen Christ John 20:26–28
Jesus appears to 500 people at the same time 1 Corinthians 15:6
Jesus instructs Peter as Jesus prepares to leave his disciples John 21:15–22
Jesus gives the Great Commission and ascends to heaven Luke 24:50–53

AD 29

AD 30

Beliefs about Jesus

Belief	Meaning	Scripture	Importance
God's Unity	There is only one God.	Deuteronomy 6:4 Exodus 20:2–3 Isaiah 43:10–11	God is eternal—he has always existed. There is one Creator of the universe.
Trinity	There is only one God, but he exists eternally in three Persons: Father, Son (Jesus), and Holy Spirit.	Matthew 3:16–17 Matthew 28:19 2 Corinthians 13:14	As Trinity, God's nature is relational and in unity.
Christ's Virgin Birth	God the Son became a human being through a supernatural conception in the Virgin Mary's womb.	Matthew 1:18–23	Jesus did not inherit the sin nature that all other human beings have.
Christ's Sinlessness	Jesus never sinned.	2 Corinthians 5:21 Hebrews 4:15 1 Peter 2:22	Christ's sinlessness means he is able to represent us before God and to provide our salvation.
Christ's Deity	Jesus Christ is, in essence, God. He was not just a wise teacher or a good man—he is God.	John 1:1 Colossians 2:9 Hebrews 1:8	Because Jesus is both God and human he is able to mediate between God and humankind. He is the only way for us to be restored spiritually to God.
Christ's Humanity	Jesus Christ was fully human and fully divine.	John 1:14 Philippians 2:7–8 Hebrews 2:14	Jesus is able to fully represent humanity in atonement. If Jesus were not human, he could not have paid the price for humanity's sin.

Belief	Meaning	Scripture	Importance
Christ's Atoning Death	Christ's sacrificial death on the cross and his bodily resurrection can bring us to God.	Mark 10:45 1 Peter 2:24 1 Peter 3:18 John 14:6	Jesus' death on the cross paid the penalty for humanity's sin—both physical and spiritual death.
Christ's Bodily Resurrection	Jesus rose bodily from the grave.	Romans 4:25 Romans 10:9 Luke 24:39	Jesus' resurrection from the dead was proof that he conquered death. It showed that someday everyone will be resurrected and spend eternity in either heaven or hell.
The Necessity of Faith	Faith in God and Jesus Christ, not our good works, connect us to God.	Hebrews 11:6 Romans 4:5	We cannot save ourselves because we can never repay the debt owed to God, no matter how many good things we do. Faith is trusting that God will save us through Christ's sacrifice. In faith, we accept God's gift of salvation.
Christ's Intercession	Christ represents us before God.	Hebrews 1:3 Hebrews 4:15 Hebrews 7:25 1 John 2:1	Jesus acts on our behalf. He defends us before God's law and against the accusations of Satan.
Christ's Second Coming	Jesus will return again.	Matthew 24:30 Revelation 22:12 Colossians 3:3–4 Luke 12:40	When Christ returns everyone will see him. Believers will rule with him in his kingdom forever. Those who do not believe will be separated from God forever.

Christ's Deity

Traits Unique to God	Traits of Jesus
Creation is "the work of his hands" —alone (Genesis 1:1; Psalm 102:25; Isaiah 44:24)	Creation is "the work of his hands" —all things created in and through him (John 1:3; Colossians 1:16; Hebrews 1:2, 10)
"The first and the last" (Isaiah 44:6)	"The first and the last" (Revelation 1:17; 22:13)
"Lord of lords" (Deuteronomy 10:17; Psalm 136:3)	"Lord of lords" (1 Timothy 6:15; Revelation 17:14; 19:16)
Unchanging and eternal (Psalm 90:2; 102:26, 27; Malachi 3:6)	Unchanging and eternal (John 8:58; Colossians 1:17; Hebrews 1:11-12; 13:8)
Judge of all people (Genesis 18:25; Psalms 94:2; 96:13; 98:9)	Judge of all people (John 5:22; Acts 17:31; 2 Cor. 5:10; 2 Timothy 4:1)
Only Savior; no other God can save (Isaiah 43:11; 45:21, 22; Hosea 13:4)	Savior of the world; no salvation apart from him (John 4:42; Acts 4:12; Titus 2:13; 1 John 4:14)
Redeems from their sins a people for his own possession (Exodus 19:5; Psalm 130:7, 8; Ezekiel 37:23)	Redeems from their sins a people for his own possession (Titus 2:14)
Hears and answers prayers of those who call on him (Psalm 86:5-8; Isaiah 55:6, 7; Jer. 33:3; Joel 2:32)	Hears and answers prayers of those who call on him (John 14:14; Romans 10:12, 13; 1 Corinthians 1:2; 2 Corinthians 12:8, 9)
Only God has divine glory (Isaiah 42:8, 48:11)	Jesus has divine glory (John 17:5)
Worshipped by angels (Psalm 97:7)	Worshipped by angels (Hebrews 1:6)

Jesus:
Fact & Fiction

Was Jesus of Nazareth a Mythical Figure?
Where Was Jesus During the "Lost Years"?
Did Archaeologists Find Jesus' Bones?

Introduction

Since the 18th century, a number of scholars have questioned the testimony of the Gospels about Jesus. Today, many people are familiar with some of the criticisms these scholars raise. The issues are explored in books, articles, web sites, even television shows and movies. The criticisms have been repeated so often that many people accept them without question. Since most people are not trained in philosophy, theology, or history, the issues may seem to be mere matters of opinion.

In the following pages we will explore some of the most common misconceptions, which we call fictions, about Jesus. The purpose is to provide information and insight about the origin, reasoning, and validity of some of these popular fictions. Although some arguments and historical evidence are presented, this work is not a formal dialogue with experts in the field. Rather, it is an introductory resource for believers who may be struggling with some of these questions, or people who are exploring the Christian faith but still have doubts.

A brief word about the historical reliability of the New Testament may be helpful. Modern science does not really prove or disprove miracles. However, history, archaeology, and other social sciences have shown the New Testament to be historically accurate and reliable. These are a few of the reasons for this confidence:

> ➤ The New Testament writings were based on eyewitness testimony.

> ➤ There are many documents from writers as early as the late first century AD which confirm various details of the New Testament accounts.

> ➤ The existence of many early manuscripts allows us to be confident that the New Testament was accurately copied.

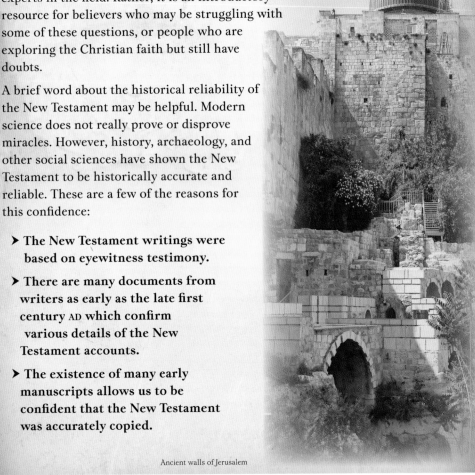

Ancient walls of Jerusalem

Is Jesus of Nazareth a mythical person?

FICTION: Jesus probably didn't exist.

Some people argue that Jesus either did not exist or was so unlike the person described in the New Testament that we cannot know anything about him. "Historically, it is quite doubtful whether Christ ever existed at all, and if He did we do not know anything about Him" (Bertrand Russell, philosopher). "It is easier to account for the facts of early Christian history if Jesus were a fiction than if he once were real" (Frank R. Zindler, atheist activist).

FACT: Historical data confirm that the Gospel testimonies are reliable and accurate.

Historians agree that Jesus existed. Robert J. Miller, a skeptical historian, writes, "We can be certain that Jesus really existed (despite a few hyper-historical skeptics who refuse to be convinced)." Biblical scholar F. F. Bruce stated, "The historicity of Christ is as axiomatic [certain, unchallenged fact] for an unbiased historian as the historicity of Julius Caesar."

Many historical documents from around the time Jesus lived confirm the existence of Jesus. Along with the New Testament, there are references to Jesus in the writings of first-century and early second-century writers, such as Josephus (Jewish) and Tacitus and Pliny the Younger (Roman). No ancient writer who was opposed to Christianity questioned the historical existence of Jesus. The abundant data from the first century makes it highly possible—more than could be said of many other historical events—that the New Testament testimony is accurate.

Evidence from the Bible

Luke claimed that his Gospel was based on information handed down from "eyewitnesses" and on his own careful investigation (Luke 1:1–4). Likewise, the Gospel of John claims to be written by the very "disciple whom Jesus loved" (John 21:20–25; see also 2 Peter 1:16). Biblical authors understood the difference between history and myth, between fact and legend; they insisted that what they taught was literal, historical fact (see also 1 Corinthians 15:1–11; 2 Timothy 4:3–4).

Writing some twenty years after Jesus died, the apostle Paul mentions the following information about Jesus:

- Jesus' twelve apostles, specifically Peter (Cephas), James, and John (1 Corinthians 15:5, 7; Galatians 1:8–9).
- The Last Supper (1 Corinthians 11:23–26).
- Jesus' death and burial (1 Corinthians 15:3–4; 1 Thessalonians 2:13–16).
- Jesus' resurrection and appearances (1 Corinthians 15:5–8).
- At least some of Jesus' teachings (e.g., 1 Corinthians 9:14; cf. Luke 10:7).

Do the "Gnostic gospels" tell the real story of Jesus?

FICTION: The Gnostic gospels provide new light on the historical Jesus.

In recent years, interest in the "lost gospels"—ancient books about Jesus not included in the New Testament—has increased dramatically, thanks to books and movies like *The Da Vinci Code*. However, since 1945, when most of these lost gospels were discovered, many scholars have looked to these gospels outside the New Testament for alternative views of Jesus. Some of these scholars claim that the lost gospels portray more accurately who Jesus was.

The most significant of these ancient writings are the Gnostic gospels, which reinterpreted Jesus' life and teaching more than a century after his death. The word "Gnostic" comes from the Greek word *gnosis* ("knowledge") and refers to the Gnostics' claim to have secret information about Jesus. Gnostics generally believed that one or more semi-divine beings inferior to the true God created the world and trapped spirits in physical bodies. They also believed that salvation consisted of using their secret knowledge to escape the physical realm and unite with God.

The controversial Jesus Seminar scholars included one of the lost gospels, the *Coptic Gospel of Thomas*, in their book *The Five Gospels*—and accepted more of its sayings of Jesus than those found in the Gospel of John.

FACT: The Gnostic gospels don't provide any helpful information about the historical Jesus.

The Gnostic gospels do not include eyewitness testimony about Jesus. The New Testament gospels appeared in the first century, while people who knew Jesus might still be alive; the Gnostic gospels came out in the second century or even later. All scholars agree that it is certain that Thomas, Peter, and Judas did not actually write the "gospels" that bear their names.

Moreover, the purpose of the Gnostic gospels was to communicate Gnostic beliefs—which contradict both the Old and New Testaments—rather than to convey concrete information about Jesus' life.

Evidence from the Bible

Since the Gnostic gospels appeared years later, there is no direct response to Gnostic claims about Jesus in the New Testament (though the epistles of Colossians and 1 John address ideas that the Gnostics developed more fully). But the New Testament writings did claim to have been based on the testimonies of eyewitnesses of Jesus' life, ministry, death, and resurrection (see Luke 1:1–4; John 19:35; 21:24–25; Acts 1:21–26; 10:36–42; 1 Corinthians 9:1; 15:3–8; Galatians 1:11–12; 1 John 1:1–4). Paul recognized that other interpretations of Jesus' life and identity would arise; he warned believers to be on guard (2 Corinthians 11:4).

Did the early church borrow the Virgin Birth story from paganism?

FICTION: Pagan society had many stories of miraculous virgin births.

Some scholars, and even some people in the church, argue that the Virgin Birth is probably a myth or legend.

James Tabor writes, "The assumption of the historian is that all human beings have both a biological mother and father, and that Jesus is no exception." Similarly, John Drury, Oxford University chaplain, remarks, "Virgin births were a rather Gentile thing. You get it in a lot of the legends in Ovid where the god impregnates some young girl who has a miraculous son."

FACT: The birth of Jesus was a special, unique event in history.

Because of the very private nature of conception and pregnancy, it is impossible to prove the Virgin Birth historically. However, it is possible to show that there are good reasons to accept the event as historical fact.

Most importantly, the pagan stories are not about "virgin births" at all. As some scholars admit, in pagan myths the gods impregnated women by having sexual relations with them. Tabor agrees, "In that sense the account [in the Gospels] is different from those miraculous birth stories so common in Greco-Roman mythology." Skeptics like Gerd Lüdemann (an atheist scholar) and John Shelby Spong (the former Episcopal bishop of Newark), following the feminist scholar Jane Schaberg, take the view that Jesus was Mary's illegitimate child. However, the Gospels of Matthew and Luke, which report the Virgin Birth, were written in the first century—still within the lifetime of family members and others who had known Jesus personally.

Evidence from the Bible

"This is how the birth of Jesus Christ came about: his mother Mary was pledged to be married to Joseph, but before they came together, she was found to be with child through the Holy Spirit" (Matthew 1:18).

The dialogue between the angel and Mary in Luke 1:30–37 makes it clear that:

- Mary was a virgin.

- Jesus' birth was a special act of the Holy Spirit.

Orazio Gentleschi (1563-1639)–*Annunciation*

Where was Jesus during his "lost years"?

FICTION: Jesus was trained by gurus in the East.

People have often wondered why the New Testament does not offer more details about Jesus' life, especially between the ages of twelve and thirty. Some suggest that Jesus traveled far and wide during these so-called "lost years" to learn from other religious leaders.

At the end of the 18th century, a wealthy Russian explorer, Nicolas Notovitch, claimed to have discovered an ancient Buddhist manuscript. This manuscript described how Jesus lived and studied around India.

Today, some New Age teachers cite this story to support their claim that Jesus taught something more like Buddhism than Christianity. For example, actress and author Shirley MacLaine claims that Jesus was "traveling in and around India and Tibet and Persia and the Near East" and was trained as a "yogi" before returning to Galilee.

FACT: There is no basis in fact for the claim that Jesus studied in the East.

No ancient document—not even any of the "gospels" that were not included in the New Testament—affirms that Jesus ever lived or traveled outside the land of Israel, except for his infancy in Egypt (Matthew 2).

The most frequently cited source for the claim that Jesus went East is Notovitch's book *The Unknown Life of Jesus Christ*. Notovitch's claims were strongly questioned from the beginning. For example:

- During Jesus' lifetime, the main religion in Tibet was the Bön religion (a form of shamanism), not Buddhism.
- Although Notovitch did travel to Tibet, Archibald Douglas, a British professor, proved in 1895 that Notovitch had not visited the monastery in question.
- Douglas also showed that the monastery did not have a manuscript mentioning Jesus.

Evidence from the Bible

Although the Gospels do not report on Jesus' specific activities between the ages of twelve and thirty, they do tell us enough to discount the theory that Jesus was studying Buddhism in the East during those years.

The Gospels also report that people in Jesus' hometown of Nazareth knew him as a carpenter, a trade he learned from Joseph (Matthew 13:55; Mark 6:3), which suggests that Jesus spent his young adult years there. After his baptism and time in the desert, "Jesus returned to Galilee," went to Nazareth, "and on the Sabbath day he went into the synagogue, as was his custom" (Luke 4:14–16).

5 Can we become the Christ?

FICTION: Jesus was just a man who realized his "Christ consciousness."

As some Eastern religions have become more influential in the West, many people have reinterpreted Christian terms using Eastern concepts. For example, the New Age movement and Mind-Science groups (such as Christian Science and Unity) interpret "Christ" to mean "the divine that is in all of us." In this view, Jesus was just a man who attained "Christ consciousness"—a realization of oneness with the divine that is the potential in all human beings. For example: "We are all manifestations of Buddha consciousness, or Christ consciousness, only we don't know it. The word 'Buddha' means 'the one who waked up.' We are all to do that—to wake up to the Christ or Buddha consciousness within us" (Joseph Campbell, professor of mythology).

FACT: Only Jesus qualifies to be "the Christ."

The title "Christ" (Greek, *christos*) means "anointed one." The "Christ" was the anointed king who would fulfill God's promises to David of an eternal kingdom of justice and peace through one of his descendants. Jesus, a descendant of David, claimed to be that anointed one (Luke 4:16–21). Although various individuals in the Old Testament (such as King David) were anointed to their offices, there could only be one divinely anointed king of God's people. Similarly, all believers are said to have an "anointing" from God (1 John 2:20–27), but the New Testament recognizes only Jesus as "the Christ."

The concept of a universal "Christ consciousness" is a modern creation; it may be compatible with some forms of Buddhism, but it is *not* a Christian idea.

Evidence from the Bible

Jesus said, "For many will come in my name, claiming, 'I am the Christ,' and will deceive many" (Matthew 24:5).

"The woman said, 'I know that Messiah' (called Christ) 'is coming. When he comes, he will explain everything to us.' Then Jesus declared, 'I who speak to you am he'" (John 4:25–26).

"But these are written that you may believe that Jesus is the Christ, the Son of God, and that by believing you may have life in his name" (John 20:31).

Was Jesus married?

FICTION: The church conspired to conceal Jesus' marriage.

The idea that Jesus was married became especially popular after Dan Brown's novel *The Da Vinci Code*, which claims, "The marriage of Jesus and Mary Magdalene is part of the historical record."

James Tabor argues that the silence of the Gospels about Jesus' wife is no more significant than their silence about the wives of Jesus' brothers and apostles: "They are simply not considered important to the story, but it does not mean they did not exist." Others argue that all Jewish rabbis were married, and therefore, since Jesus was a rabbi, he must have been married at some point.

Writers who claim that Jesus and Mary Magdalene were husband and wife think this is implied in some of the Gnostic gospels. For example, the *Gospel of Philip* (probably written in the third century AD) makes some sort of statement about Jesus kissing Mary, which many interpret as proof they were married.

FACT: There is no evidence that Jesus was married.

The arguments marshaled by proponents of this view do not support their case:

- Sections of the only existing copy of the *Gospel of Philip* are greatly damaged and difficult to read clearly. We should be hesitant to derive any confident conclusions from this fragmented sentence in a document dating two centuries after Jesus.

- Most scholars agree that the "kiss" here refers to a religious, mystical ritual of some sort involving a kiss.

- As scientist Charles Pellegrino (who claims that Jesus and Mary were married) admits: "In none of the Gospels, be they canonical or apocryphal, is Mary Magdalene—*Mariamne*—described as being married to Jesus."

- While rabbis generally frowned on men not marrying, they acknowledged that there could be exceptions, notably for prophets. Some groups of Jews at the time of Jesus (such as the Essenes) actually encouraged celibacy.

Evidence from the Bible

The Gospels mention many of Jesus' relatives, including father, mother, brothers, sisters, and cousins, but no wife or children. Their silence about whether Jesus was married, then, is at least good evidence that he was not.

The Bible makes it clear that Jesus' mission was to redeem people from sin so that they could become God's adopted children (Matthew 5:9; 6:9; 7:11; 23:8–9; Mark 3:33–35; Romans 8:14–23, 29; Galatians 4:4–7). He dedicated his life to this mission of redemption. Perhaps this is why Jesus did not get married and start a family.

Did Jesus die on the cross?

FICTION: Jesus somehow avoided——or survived—— crucifixion.

A surprisingly large number of people in the world know something about Jesus but think that he did not really die on the cross.

According to the *Qur'an*, the scripture of Islam, the Jews claimed to have killed Jesus, but "they slew him not nor crucified him, but it appeared so unto them." Many Muslims think someone else—perhaps even Judas—was crucified instead.

Others agree that Jesus was crucified but speculate that he survived the ordeal, perhaps merely passing out on the cross (the "swoon theory"). Conspiracy theorist Michael Baigent asserts that when Mark reports that Joseph of Arimathea asked Pilate permission to bury Jesus' "body," Mark uses the Greek word *soma*—which, he claims, means a live body, not a corpse (Mark 15:43). Baigent concludes: "Jesus' survival is revealed right there in the Gospel account."

FACT: Jesus died on the cross.

The claim that someone other than Jesus died on the cross has no historical evidence to support it. Friends and family members, including his mother Mary, witnessed his crucifixion (Luke 23:49–56; John 19:25–27, 38–42). The Jewish leaders had seen Jesus in Jerusalem for several days, and they would certainly have known and objected if the Romans were crucifying the wrong man.

Caravaggio (1571–1610)—*The Entombment*

Baigent is mistaken: the word *soma* can refer either to a live body or to a corpse (for example, Luke 17:37; Acts 9:40; Romans 8:10). The swoon theory picks and chooses select elements of the Gospel accounts and takes them out of context:

- Pilate was surprised that Jesus had perished so quickly (Mark 15:44a), since crucifixion victims usually took days to die. However, Mark also tells us that Pilate checked with the centurion who oversaw Jesus' execution and verified that he was in fact dead (15:44b–45).

- When a soldier pierced Jesus' body with a spear, "blood and water came out" (John 19:34), supposedly proving that he was still alive. Medical experts have offered several suggestions as to the source of the blood and water, all consistent with Jesus' already being dead. In any case, had Jesus not quite been dead, stabbing him with a spear so that he lost still more blood would surely have finished the job.

Even skeptic and scholar John Dominic Crossan has stated: "Jesus' death by execution under Pontius Pilate is as sure as anything historical can ever be."

Did archaeologists find Jesus' bones?

FICTION: The "Jesus family tomb" belonged to Jesus.

Simcha Jacobovici, a journalist specializing in biblical archaeological news, and Charles Pellegrino, a science writer, claimed in 2007 that they had found the tomb in which Jesus, his mother Mary, brother Joseph, wife Mary Magdalene, and son Judah were buried.

Israeli authorities warehouse hundreds of ossuaries—limestone boxes in which first-century Jews buried the dried-out bones of the deceased. Among the ossuaries found in a tomb in Talpiot (a Jerusalem suburb) were ones inscribed with the names "Jesus son of Joseph," "Jose," "Maria," "Judah son of Jesus," "Matia," and one with a disputed inscription that some say reads "Mariamne also known as Mara." Jacobovici and Pellegrino claim this means "Mary the Master" and identify her as Mary Magdalene, whom some Christians regarded as a spiritual authority.

Jacobovici and Pellegrino concluded that the Talpiot tomb was the final resting place of the bones of Jesus Christ.

FACT: The tomb doesn't belong to Jesus or his family.

Despite the popularity of the idea, virtually no biblical scholar (other than James Tabor) has endorsed the "Jesus family tomb" theory. One of the main reasons is that "Jesus" and "Joseph" were very common names in the first century, as was "Mary" (about one out of four women had that name).

The "Jesus family tomb" theory depends largely on identifying one of the Marys as Mary Magdalene, but this is the argument's weakest point. The inscription either says "Mary also known as Mara" or "Mary and Mara"—and Mara was another name for Martha. In this context, the meaning "Master" is highly unlikely. And no ancient text calls Mary Magdalene a "Master." Since we are reasonably sure Jesus Christ did not have a wife or son, we can confidently reject the Talpiot tomb as belonging to him.

Evidence from the Bible

The Gospels report that Jesus' body was buried in the tomb of Joseph of Arimathea in the late afternoon before the Sabbath (Mark 15:42–47). Early on the morning of the Sabbath, several of his women followers went to the tomb to anoint the body and discovered the tomb empty. An angel at the tomb told the women, "Don't be alarmed.... You are looking for Jesus the Nazarene, who was crucified. He has risen! He is not here. See the place where they laid him" (Mark 16:6).

Joseph's tomb was empty because Jesus had risen from the dead, not because his body had been moved to another tomb.

Did Jesus rise from the grave?

FICTION: The resurrection of Jesus is merely a pious legend.

Skeptics discount the resurrection of Jesus as a miracle—and they typically reject the possibility of miracles altogether.

"If you say that Jesus rose from the dead biologically, you would have to presuppose that a decaying corpse—which is already cold and without blood in its brain—could be made alive again. I think that is nonsense" (Gerd Lüdemann, professor of early Christianity).

The belief that Jesus rose physically from the dead "is exactly like the belief in Santa's visiting every child's home throughout the earth during a single evening" (Robert M. Price, professor of theology).

FACT: The available evidence strongly suggests that Jesus' resurrection was a fact.

If Jesus' resurrection were a legend, the Jewish authorities would not have accused Jesus' disciples of having stolen the body. Hundreds of people personally saw the risen Jesus. These eyewitnesses suffered persecution and, in some cases, martyrdom for these stories.

To reject the possibility of miracles is to make a philosophical assumption, not something that skeptics can prove through science or history. Skeptical explanations (such as the "swoon theory" or the claim the disciples suffered a mass hallucination) simply do not work. In the words of New Testament scholar N.T. Wright, "Once you allow that something remarkable happened to the body that morning, all the other data fall into place with ease. Once you insist that nothing so outlandish happened, you are driven to ever more complex and fantastic hypotheses."

The best explanation for all of the known facts is that Jesus did in fact rise from the dead.

Evidence from the Bible

The Gospels report that Jesus died, that he was buried in a rock tomb, and that women followers of Jesus discovered the tomb to be empty a couple of days later (Matt. 28:1–7), a fact confirmed by male followers (Luke 24:12; John 20:3–10). Jesus appeared alive to some of those same women (Matthew 28:8–10; John 20:11–18). He also appeared to his apostles (Luke 24:34; 1 Corinthians 15:5, 7; Matthew 28:16–20; Luke 24:36–49; John 20:19–29). On one occasion he appeared to more than five hundred (1 Corinthians 15:6). He even appeared to Saul (Paul), a rabbi who had fiercely opposed the Christian faith (Acts 9:1-9; 1 Corinthians 15:8).

Is Jesus the only way to God?

FICTION: Jesus is merely one of the world's many religious leaders.

Many people argue that while belief in Jesus is fine for some, it is intolerant—even hateful—to say that Jesus is the only way to know God, the only way of salvation.

Oprah Winfrey, in response to a member of her studio audience who argued that Jesus was the only way to God, replied, "There couldn't *possibly* be only one way."

New Age teacher Deepak Chopra claims, "I want to offer the possibility that Jesus was truly, as he proclaimed, a savior. Not the savior, not the one and only Son of God. Rather, Jesus embodied the highest level of enlightenment."

FACT: Jesus claimed to be the exclusive way to God and salvation.

If Jesus had been merely a religious and ethical teacher, he might even have been the best such teacher—but by no means the only one. When people criticize the notion that Jesus is the only way, they are typically thinking of Jesus as a teacher or guru, an enlightened master or a spiritual role model. However, this is not an adequate understanding of who or what Jesus is. Jesus made claims about himself and performed wonders that no one else did:

1. He is the Son of God.

2. He lived a sinless life, raised the dead, gave sight to the blind.

3. He died as a substitute for the sins of the world, so that we may have eternal life in God's kingdom.

4. He will be the Judge at the end of history, determining who receives eternal life and who does not.

These claims are either extremely arrogant and delusional, or true.

Evidence from the Bible

"Jesus answered, 'I am the way and the truth and the life. No one comes to the Father except through me'" (John 14:6).

"Salvation is found in no one else, for there is no other name under heaven given to men by which we must be saved" (Acts 4:12).

"Therefore God exalted him to the highest place and gave him the name that is above every name, that at the name of Jesus every knee should bow, in heaven and on earth and under the earth, and every tongue confess that Jesus Christ is Lord, to the glory of God the Father" (Philippians 2:9–11).

Is Jesus God?

The New Testament teaches that Jesus is God:

- It explicitly refers to him as "God" (John 1:1; 20:28; Titus 2:13; Hebrews 1:8; 2 Peter 1:1).

- It gives him other divine titles, such as "Lord"—often in contexts where this title clearly stands for the Old Testament name Yahweh (Romans 10:9–13, see Joel 2:32; Philippians 2:9–11; Isaiah 45:23).

- Jesus is the King of kings and Lord of lords (Revelation 17:14; 19:16; see Daniel 4:37).

- He is the first and the last, the beginning and the end, the Alpha and Omega (Revelation 1:7–8, 17b–18; 2:8; 22:13–14; see Isaiah 41:4; 44:6; 48:12).

- It describes him as having divine attributes, such as having no beginning (John 1:1–3; Colossians 1:16–17), existing everywhere at the same time (Matthew 18:20; 28:20), and being absolutely loving (Romans 8:35–39; Ephesians 3:19).

- It credits him with doing God's works, such as creating and sustaining the world (John 1:3; Colossians 1:16–17; Hebrews 1:2–3, 10). Jesus forgave sins (Mark 2:1–12) and claimed that he will pass final judgment on all people (John 5:22–23).

- It accords all divine honors to him (John 5:23): worship (Matthew 28:17; Hebrews 1:6), prayer (John 14:14; 1 Corinthians 1:2; Revelation 22:20–21), and reverence (Ephesians 5:21).

Principal Author: Robert M. Bowman, Jr., Director of the Institute for Religious Research (IRR), MA in Biblical Studies and Theology

General Editor: Paul Carden, Executive Director, Centers for Apologetics Research (CFAR)

Notes

Q 1: Bertrand Russell, "Why I Am Not a Christian," in *Why I Am Not a Christian and Other Essays on Religion and Related Subjects* (Touchstone, 1967), 16; Frank R. Zindler, "Did Jesus Exist?" *American Atheist*, Summer 1998; F. F. Bruce, *The New Testament Documents: Are They Reliable?* (IVP, 1960), 119.
Robert J. Miller, "Back to Basics: A Primer on Historical Method," in *Finding the Historical Jesus: Rules of Evidence*, ed. Bernard Brandon Scott, Jesus Seminar Guides (Santa Rosa, CA: Polebridge Press, 2008), 10.

Q 3: James D. Tabor, *The Jesus Dynasty* (Simon & Schuster, 2006), 59, 45; John Drury, quoted in *Time*, 12/8/04; Gerd Lüdemann, *Virgin Birth?* (Trinity Press Intl., 1998), 51–65; Jane Schaberg, *The Illegitimacy of Jesus* (Harper, 1987).

Q 4: Shirley MacLaine, *Out on a Limb* (Bantam, 1984), 233–34; J. Archibald Douglas, "The Chief Lama of Himis on the Alleged 'Unknown Life of Christ,'" *The Nineteenth Century*, 39 (January-June 1896): 667–77.

Q 5: Joseph Campbell, *The Power of Myth*, with Bill Moyers (Anchor Books, 1991), 69.

Q 6: Dan Brown, *The Da Vinci Code* (Doubleday, 2003), 234, 245, 317; James Tabor, "Was Jesus Married?" (http://jesusdynasty.com/blog/); Simcha Jacobovici and Charles Pellegrino, *The Jesus Family Tomb* (HarperSanFrancisco, 2007), 105.

Q 7: Qur'an 4:157–58; Michael Baigent, *The Jesus Papers* (HarperCollins, 2006), 130; Matthew W. Maslen and Piers D. Mitchell, "Medical Theories on the Cause of Death in Crucifixion," *Journal of the Royal Society of Medicine* 99 (2006): 185–88; John Dominic Crossan, *Who Killed Jesus?* (Harper, 1995), 5.

Q 8: Jacobovici and Pellegrino, *Jesus Family Tomb*; James Tabor, http://jesusdynasty.com/blog/.

Q 9: *Jesus' Resurrection: Fact or Figment? A Debate Between William Lane Craig & Gerd Lüdemann*, ed. Paul Copan and Ronald K. Tacelli (IVP, 2000), 45; "Introduction," in *The Empty Tomb: Jesus Beyond the Grave*, ed. Robert M. Price and Jeffery Jay Lowder (Prometheus, 2005), 12; *The Meaning of Jesus: Two Visions*, by N. T. Wright and Marcus Borg (SPCK, 1999), 124.

Q 10: "The Gospel According to Oprah," www.wfial.org; Deepak Chopra, *The Third Jesus: The Christ We Cannot Ignore* (Harmony, 2008).

Recommended Reading

Note: The inclusion of a work does not necessarily mean endorsement of all its contents or of other works by the same author(s).

Bauckham, Richard. *Jesus and the Eyewitnesses.* Eerdmans, 2006.

Blomberg, Craig L. *The Historical Reliability of the Gospels.* 2d ed. IVP, 2008.

Bock, Darrell L. *The Missing Gospels.* Thomas Nelson, 2007.

Bock, Darrell L., and Daniel B. Wallace. *Dethroning Jesus: Exposing Popular Culture's Quest to Unseat the Biblical Christ.* Thomas Nelson, 2007.

Bowman, Robert M., Jr., and J. Ed Komoszewski. *Putting Jesus in His Place: The Case for the Deity of Christ.* Kregel, 2007.

Bruce, F. F. *The New Testament Documents: Are They Reliable?* 6th ed. Eerdmans/IVP, 1981.

Eddy, Paul Rhodes, and Gregory A. Boyd. *The Jesus Legend: A Case for the Historical Reliability of the Synoptic Jesus Tradition.* Baker, 2007. Advanced study.

Edwards, James R. *Is Jesus the Only Savior?* Eerdmans, 2005.

Evans, Craig A. *Fabricating Jesus.* IVP, 2006.

Geivett, R. Douglas, and Gary R. Habermas, eds. *In Defense of Miracles.* IVP, 1997.

Groothuis, Douglas R. *Jesus in an Age of Controversy.* Wipf & Stock, 2002.

Habermas, Gary R., and Michael R. Licona. *The Case for the Resurrection of Jesus.* Kregel, 2004.

Hengel, Martin. *Crucifixion in the Ancient World and the Folly of the Message of the Cross.* Fortress, 1977. Advanced study.

Jenkins, Philip. *Hidden Gospels: How the Search for Jesus Lost Its Way.* Oxford, 2002.

Jones, Timothy Paul. *Misquoting Truth: A Guide to the Fallacies of Bart Ehrman's "Misquoting Jesus".* IVP, 2007.

Komoszewski, J. Ed, M. James Sawyer, and Daniel B. Wallace. *Reinventing Jesus.* Kregel, 2006.

Pate, C. Marvin, and Sheryl Lynn Pate. *Crucified in the Media: Finding the Real Jesus Amidst Today's Headlines.* Baker, 2005.

Quarles, Charles, ed. *Buried Hope or Risen Savior? The Search for the Jesus Tomb.* Broadman & Holman, 2008.

Roberts, Mark D. *Can We Trust the Gospels?* Crossway, 2007.

Strobel, Lee. *The Case for the Real Jesus.* Zondervan, 2007.

Van Voorst, Robert E. *Jesus Outside the New Testament.* Eerdmans, 2000. Advanced study.

Gospels
Side by Side

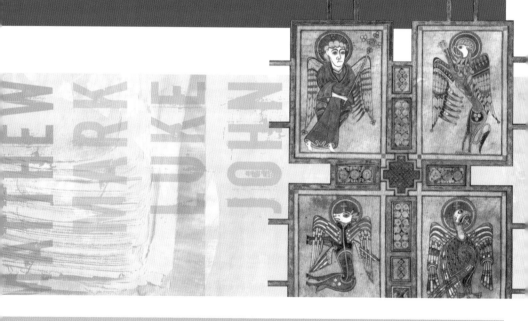

A Harmony of the Gospels
of the Life of Jesus

Why Do We Need Four Gospels?

Because the four Gospels contain different accounts of the same or similar events in the life of Jesus, readers of the Gospels have often sought to compare and contrast these accounts by placing them next to each other. These side-by-side comparisons attempt to harmonize the work of the four Evangelists and so are often called "Gospel Harmonies."

FOUR POINTS OF VIEW

Gospel	Symbol	Viewpoint	Audience	Jesus the Son of God
Matthew	Lion	Palestinian Jewish	Jewish world	Is the Messiah King of Israel
Mark	Bull	Hellenistic Jewish	Greek-speaking world	Is the Power of God in the world
Luke	Man	Greco-Roman	Gentile world	Is the Ideal Man of God
John	Eagle	Heavenly	Whole world	Is the Word of God

Why are there four Gospels instead of just one? One answer is that it takes four points of view to get the whole story about Jesus. Some might argue that one authoritative story should be enough. However, God chose to reveal himself using four Gospels. The Gospel of John begins with these words: "In the beginning was the Word ... (vs. 1) and the Word became flesh ... (vs. 14). In other words, God chooses as his preferred method of communication to speak to humans by means of the human. This is true of the Bible and it is supremely true of Christ whom we are told is God in the flesh (John 1:14–18). So then, the Gospels are, like Jesus, both a Divine work as well as a human work. They have real human authors and one divine Author. They give details that might be difficult to understand, but they are never truly contradictory. They have four different points of view on the history of Jesus but only one Divine conclusion as to his identity as the Son of God.

The Gospels as Biography

The four Gospels are best understood as biographies about the life and times of Jesus. However, there are important differences between modern and ancient biographies. The main difference is the notion of *historical sequencing*.

MODERN BIOGRAPHIES	ANCIENT BIOGRAPHIES
• Biographies written today place a premium on sequencing. • The events of the subject's life are typically narrated in the order in which they happened. • Beginning with the birth of the individual, relevant events and information are viewed in sequential order up to the death of the subject. • While chapters may present different phases in the subject's life, these phases are arranged in the order in which they are supposed to have happened.	• Ancient biographers had a general commitment to an historical sequence. • They did not feel the need to place every detail in their writings in the exact order in which it happened. • Much more emphasis is given to developing an accurate picture of the character of the subject. Deeds and happenings are seen as illustrative of that character no matter when they occurred.

THE GOSPELS AS BIOGRAPHIES

• Luke 7:36–50 is an example of the non-sequential nature of ancient biographies.
• This passage is Luke's account of the woman who anoints Jesus' feet.
• Matthew, Mark and John tell this event as part of Jesus' arrival at Bethany just before the events of Easter week (see Harmony Chart).
• Despite Luke's care as an accurate historian (Luke 1:1–4), he places this event much earlier in Jesus' ministry—that is, if we read Luke like we would read a modern biography.
• Some have tried to resolve the difficulty by suggesting that there were two such events, two times when various women anointed Jesus' feet. But the details of Luke's account too closely resemble the other Gospel accounts to make it a separate incident.
• It is much more likely that Luke (and so the Holy Spirit) was simply using this event out of historical sequence to illustrate the Pharisees and their lack of faith in contrast to the faith of the centurion (Luke 7:2–10).

Harmony of the Gospels

EVENT	MATTHEW	MARK	LUKE	JOHN
The genealogy of Jesus	1:1–17		3:23–38	
Jesus' birth and childhood	1:18–2:23		1:5–2:52	
John the Baptist's ministry	3:1–12	1:1–8	3:1–18	1:19–34
Christ's public ministry and first Passover	3:13–4:12	1:9–14	3:21–4:13	1:35–4:42
Christ's ministry in Galilee	4:12	1:14–15	4:14–15	4:43–54
His rejection at Nazareth and move to Capernaum	4:13–22; 8:14–17	1:16–34	4:16–41	
His first ministry tour and second Passover	4:23–12:14	1:35–3:6	4:42–7:50	5:1–47
His second ministry tour	12:15–13:58	3:7–6:6	8:1–56	
His third ministry tour	9:35–11:1; 14:1–12	6:6–29	9:1–9	
Ministry to his disciples and third Passover	14:13–18:35	6:30–9:50	9:10–56	6:1–71
Ministry in Judea			10:1–13:21	7:1–10:39
Ministry beyond Jordan	19:1–20:34	10:1–52	13:22–19:27	10:40–11:54
The last week (Passover/Easter)	21:12–28:20	11:1–16:20	19:28–24:53	11:55–21:25
Arrival in Bethany and Mary anoints Jesus' feet	26:6–13	14:3–9	19:28	11:55–12:11
Triumphal entry	21:1–11	11:1–11	19:29–44	12:12–19
Second cleansing of the temple; barren fig tree cursed	21:12–13; 18–22	11:12–18	19:45–48	
Greeks seek Jesus; fig tree withered	21:19–22	11:19–25	21:37–38	12:20–50
Jesus' authority challenged	21:23–22:46	11:27–12:37	20:1–44	
Denouncing the scribes and Pharisees	23:1–39	12:38–40	20:45–47	
Widow's offering		12:41–44	21:1–4	
The Olivet discourse	24:1–25:46	13:1–37	21:5–36	
Crucifixion predicted	26:1–5	14:1–2	22:1–2	
Judas's bargain	26:14–16	14:10–11	22:3–6	
Preparation and the Passover	26:17–30	14:12–26	22:7–20	13:1–14:31
Discourse and high priestly prayer				15:1–17:26
Gethsemane	26:36–46	14:32–42	22:39–46	18:1
Betrayal, arrest, and trial	26:47–56	14:43–52	22:47–53	18:2–14

EVENT	MATTHEW	MARK	LUKE	JOHN
Jesus condemned to death and Peter's denial	26:57–75	14:53–72	22:54–65	18:15–27
Formal condemnation after dawn	27:1–2	15:1	22:66–71	
Judas's suicide	27:3–10			
Jesus' first time before Pilate	27:11–14	15:1–5	23:1–5	18:28–38
Jesus before Herod the Tetrarch			23:6–12	18:39–19:16
Jesus' second time before Pilate	27:15–26	15:6–15	23:13–25	
Soldiers mock Jesus	27:27–31	15:16–23	23:26–33	19:16–17
The crucifixion	27:32–49	15:21–36	23:26–43	19:18–29
Jesus' death	27:50–56	15:37–41	23:44–49	19:30–37
Jesus' burial	27:57–66	15:42–47	23:50–56	19:38–42
Earthquake and tomb opened	28:1–4			
Visit of women at dawn	28:5–8	16:1–3	24:1–8	20:1
Women report to the apostles; Peter and John visit the tomb			24:9–12	20:2–10
Jesus appears first to Mary Magdalene		16:9–11		20:11–18
Jesus appears to other women; the guards report to the rulers	28:9–15			
Jesus appears to two on the road to Emmaus		16:12–13	24:13–32	
Jesus appears to Peter			24:33–35	
Jesus appears to ten, Thomas absent		16:14	24:36–43	20:19–25
Jesus appears to the eleven, Thomas present				20:26–31
Jesus appears to seven on the sea of Galilee				21:1–25
Jesus appears to about five hundred at an appointed mountain in Galilee	28:16–20	16:15–18		
Jesus appears to his brother James— 1 Corinthians 15:7				
Jesus appears to his apostles again, his ascension		16:19–20	24:44–53	
Jesus appears to Paul— 1 Corinthians 15:8				

Galilee and Judea

Jesus began his public ministry in Galilee, in the northern region. He spent much, if not most of his time there. Jesus frequented Judea and Jerusalem for the required religious festivals, but it seems he only spent significant time there late in his ministry (Luke 9:51). John affirms that his safety was compromised in Judea, and that it was only under cover that Jesus made his way to Jerusalem (John 7:1–10).

Yet, even this seeming insignificant fact about Christ's life was foretold in Scripture. Matthew 4:12–17 shows us that Isaiah had prophesied hundreds of years in advance that Christ's brilliant light would shine forth in Galilee (Isaiah 9:1–2).

Jesus' Last Week

The Gospel writers center much of their attention on the last week of Jesus' ministry. The previous chart reveals that about a fourth to a half of the Gospel's material has to do with the incidents surrounding Christ's death and resurrection. This should tell us of the importance of this week in their minds. It holds the key to the central issue of the church and of all history, for in that last week, the life and death of the whole world and the whole of human history were at stake. Without the death and resurrection of Jesus there is no hope, nor can there be any salvation.

Miracles of Jesus

The Gospel of John records the least number of miracles. Most of John's miracle accounts are not in the other Gospels. John seems to have intentionally included new

material that had not previously been written down. At the same time John's focus is more on Jesus' words, his teaching, rather than on the miraculous signs Jesus did. Perhaps conscious of his readers' desire for miracle stories, John adds to his Gospel the words, "I suppose that even the world would not have room for the books that would be written" about Jesus' many other deeds (John 21:25).

MIRACLE	MATTHEW	MARK	LUKE	JOHN
Water into wine				2:1–11
Official's son healed				4:46–54
Healing of demoniac in the synagogue		1:21–28	4:33–37	
Healing of Peter's mother-in-law	8:14–17	1:29–31	4:38–39	
Many healed at sunset		1:32–34	4:40–41	
Miraculous catch of fish			5:4–11	
Healing of a leper	8:2–4	1:40–45	5:12–16	
Healing of a paralytic	9:2–8	2:1–12	5:17–26	
Healing at Bethesda				5:2–15
Withered hand healed in a synagogue	12:9–14	3:1–6	6:6–11	
Many healed	12:15–21	3:7–12	6:17–19	
Centurion's servant healed	8:5–13		7:1–10	
Widow's son raised at Nain			7:11–17	
Demon-possessed man healed	12:22–23	3:20–21		
Calming of the storm	8:23–27	4:36–41	8:23–25	
Demonic legion cast out	8:28–34	5:1–20	8:26–39	
Healing of the woman with the flow of blood	9:20–22	5:24–34	8:42–48	
Raising of Jairus' daughter	9:23–26	5:35–43	8:49–56	
Healing of two blind men	9:27–31			
Healing of a mute demoniac	9:32–34			
Many healed, feeding of five thousand	14:13–21	6:30–44	9:10–17	6:1–14
Walking on water and calming of the storm	14:22–33	6:45–52		6:16–21
Syro-Phoenician woman's daughter healed	15:21–28	7:24–30		
Deaf mute healed		7:31–37		
Many healed, feeding of four thousand	15:29–39	8:1–10		
Blind man of Bethsaida healed		8:22–26		
Healing of demoniac boy	17:14–19	9:14–29	9:37–43	
Healing of the man born blind				9:1–7
Crippled woman healed on Sabbath			13:10–13	
Healing of a man with dropsy on the Sabbath			14:2–6	
Jesus raised Lazarus				11:38–44
Ten lepers cleansed			17:11–14	
Healing of two blind men near Jericho	20:29–34	10:46–52	18:35–43	
Many healed in the temple	21:14			
Healing of the severed ear			22:51	
Resurrection	28:1–20	16:1–19	24:1–53	20:1–31
Miraculous catch of fish				21:1–8

The Parables of Jesus

A parable is a short story designed to communicate a spiritual or moral lesson using everyday experiences.

PARABLE	MATTHEW	MARK	LUKE	JOHN
The Bridegroom, Cloth and Wineskins	9:10–17	2:15–22	5:29–39	
The Sower	13:3–23	4:3–20	8:5–15	
The Lamp	5:15–16	4:21–25	8:16–18; 11:33	
The Seed Growing		4:26–29		
The Weeds	13:24–30; 36–43			
The Mustard Seed	13:31–32	4:30–32	13:18–19	
The Leaven	13:33–35		13:20–21	
The Hidden Treasure	13:44			
The Pearl of Great Price	13:45–46			
The Net	13:47–50			
The Householder	13:51–53			
On Defilement	15:1–20	7:1–23		
The Narrow Door	7:13–14		13:22–30	
The Unmerciful Servant	18:23–35			
The Good Samaritan			10:29–37	
The Friend at Midnight			11:5–10	
The Rich Fool			12:16–21	
The Waiting Servants			12:35–38	
The Watchful Householder	24:42–44		12:39–40	
The Wise Steward and the Wicked Steward	24:45–51		12:41–48	
The Fig Tree 1			13:6–9	
The Guests			14:7–11	
The Banquet			14:12–24	
The Lost Sheep	18:10–14		15:1–7	
The Lost Coin			15:8–10	
The Lost Son			15:11–32	
The Unrighteous Steward			16:1–13	
The Rich Man and Lazarus			16:19–31	
The Returning Servant			17:7–10	
The Unjust Judge and the Widow			18:1–8	
The Pharisee and Publican			18:9–14	
The Laborers in the Vineyard	20:1–16			
The Fig Tree 2	21:18–22	11:12–24		
The Ten Minas			19:11–27	
The Two Sons	21:28–32			
The Tenants	21:33–46	12:1–12	20:9–18	
The Wedding Banquet	22:1–14			
The Fig Tree 3	24:32–35	13:28–31	21:29–33	
The Ten Virgins	25:1–13			
The Talents	25:14–30			
The Sheep and the Goats	25:31–46			

Jesus' Passovers

One way to measure the length of Jesus'
public ministry is by counting the number
of Passovers the Gospels record. Since the
Passover festival only happened once a year,
counting the Passovers gives a rough idea of
how long Jesus' ministry lasted. The Gospels
suggest that Jesus' public ministry continued
for at least three years. Notice, John is the
writer most concerned to give us the details
about the festivals in Jesus life.

FEAST	EVENT OR TEACHING	SCRIPTURE
First Passover	Jesus went to the Passover. He cleansed the temple, talked with Nicodemus and ministered in Judea for a while.	John 2:13–25
Second Passover	Jesus went to the "feast" (probably Passover) and healed the man at the pool of Bethesda.	John 5:1–47
Third Passover	Jesus delivered his "Bread of Life" teaching. However, he did not go to Passover because of a threat to his life in Judea.	John 6:4–7:1
Tabernacles (Booths)	Jesus went secretly for reasons of security. Teaching in the temple, he encountered opposition from the religious leaders. Jesus claimed to be the "Light of the World." He healed the man born blind near the pool of Siloam.	John 7:2–9:41
Hanukkah (Dedication)	Jesus attended the feast. He spoke of his "sheep." Again he escaped stoning.	John 10:22–42
Last Passover/ Last Supper	Jesus went to the Passover and the last week of his life took place.	Matthew 26:17; Mark 14:12; Luke 22:7; John 12:1

Tracking Jesus' Moves

The use of this kind of harmony is also helpful to get a picture of Jesus' movements.

PLACE	EVENT OR TEACHING	SCRIPTURE
Bethlehem	Birth of Jesus	Mt. 1:24–25; Lk. 2:1–7
Egypt	Flight from Herod	Mt. 2:13–15
Nazareth	Early childhood	Mt. 2:19–23; Lk. 2:39
Jerusalem	Passover celebration	Lk. 2:41–52
Jordan River	Baptism of Jesus	Mt.3:13–17; Mk. 1:9–11; Lk. 3:21–23; Jn. 1:29–34
Wilderness	Temptation of Jesus	Mt. 4:1–11; Mk. 1:12–13; Lk. 4:1–13
Going to Galilee	Calling of Philip and Nathaniel	Jn. 1:43–51
Cana in Galilee	First miracle	Jn. 2:1–11
Capernaum	Family stay	Jn. 2:12
Jerusalem	First Passover	Jn. 2:13–25
Judea	Baptizing new disciples	Jn. 3:22
Returning to Galilee	Jesus goes through Samaria	Jn. 4:1–4
Samaria	Jesus talks to the women at the well	Jn. 4:5–42
Cana in Galilee	Healing of official's son and the beginning of Jesus' Galilean ministry	Jn. 4:43–54; Mt. 4:12; Mk. 1:14–15; Lk. 4:14–15
Nazareth	Rejection at Nazareth	Lk. 4:16–30
Capernaum	Move of ministry base	Mt. 4:13; Mk.1:21; Lk. 4:31
Galilee	Preaching tour	Mt. 4:23–25; Mk. 1:32–39; Lk. 4:42–44
Jerusalem	Second Passover	Jn. 5:1–47
Galilee	The parable of the Sower and Seed	Mt. 13:1; Mk. 4:1; Lk. 8:1–4
Gennesaret	Healing of multitudes	Mt. 14:34–36; Mk. 6:53–56
Tyre and Sidon	Faith of the Canaanite woman	Mt. 15:21–28; Mk. 7:24–30
The Region of the Decapolis	Healing of deaf and dumb man, feeding of the 4000	Mt. 15:29–38; Mk. 7:31–8:9
Galilee	Teaching and healing	Mt. 15:39–16:5; Mk. 8:10–26
Caesarea Philippi	The question of Jesus' identity	Mt. 16:13–20; Mk. 8:27–30; Lk. 9:18–21
Galilee and Capernaum	Jesus tells of his death a second time, the half-shekel tax	Mk. 17:22–27; Mk. 9:30–50
Jerusalem	Feast of Tabernacles	Lk. 9:51; Jn. 7:2–10
Various places in Judea	Preaching tour	Lk. 10:1–24
Jerusalem	Feast of Dedication (Hanukkah)	Jn. 10:22–23
Across the Jordan	Preaching tour	Mt. 19:1; Mk. 10:1; Lk. 13:22; Jn. 10:40–42
Between Galilee and Samaria	Ten lepers healed	Lk. 17:11–19
Jericho	Jesus heals blind men	Mt. 20:29–34; Mk. 10:46–52
Bethany	The raising of Lazarus	Jn. 11:1–53
Ephraim	Jesus stays with his disciples	Jn. 11:54
Bethany, Jerusalem and places in the vicinity	Jesus' last week (Passover/Easter)	Mt. 26:6–28:15; Mk. 14:3–16:11; Lk. 19:28–24:49; Jn. 11:55–20:31
Galilee	Appears to his disciples	Mt. 28:16–20; Mk. 16:15–18; Jn. 21:1–23
Mount of Olives	Jesus' ascension	Mk. 16:19–20; Lk. 24:50–53

Israel During Jesus' Time

Jesus' three-year ministry occurred all over the ancient cities. From Syria to Judea, Jesus brought the gospel's powerful words and actions.

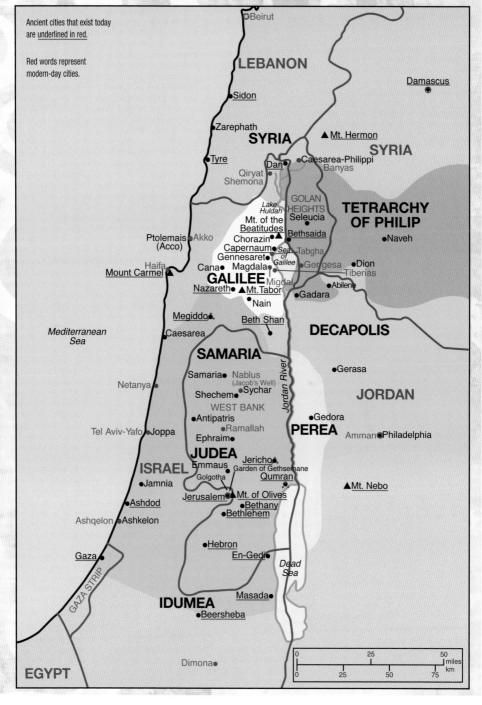

Ancient cities that exist today are underlined in red.

Red words represent modern-day cities.

Beirut
LEBANON
Damascus
Sidon
Zarephath
SYRIA
▲ Mt. Hermon
SYRIA
Tyre
Dan
Caesarea-Philippi
Banyas
Qiryat Shemona
Lake Huldah
GOLAN HEIGHTS
TETRARCHY OF PHILIP
Mt. of the Beatitudes
Seleucia
Chorazin
Bethsaida
Naveh
Ptolemais (Acco)
Akko
Capernaum
Sea of Galilee
Tabgha
Gennesaret
Gergesa
Dion
Haifa
Cana
Magdala
Tiberias
Mount Carmel
GALILEE
Migdal
Nazareth ▲ Mt. Tabor
Abilene
Gadara
Nain
Megiddo
Beth Shan
DECAPOLIS
Mediterranean Sea
Caesarea
SAMARIA
Gerasa
Samaria
Nablus (Jacob's Well)
Netanya
Shechem
Sychar
JORDAN
WEST BANK
Antipatris
Gedora
Tel Aviv-Yafo
Joppa
Ramallah
PEREA
Amman Philadelphia
Ephraim
JUDEA
Jericho
Emmaus
Garden of Gethsemane
ISRAEL
Golgotha
Qumran
Jamnia
Jerusalem
Mt. of Olives
▲ Mt. Nebo
Ashdod
Bethany
Bethlehem
Ashqelon
Ashkelon
Hebron
Gaza
En-Gedi
Dead Sea
GAZA STRIP
IDUMEA
Masada
Beersheba
EGYPT
Dimona

0		25		50
				miles
0	25		50	75
				km

The Synoptic Gospels and John

The word "synoptic" means "seen together." It refers to the first three Gospels, Matthew, Mark and Luke. When seen together, these Gospels often reveal related accounts in very similar language. Scholars agree there is some relationship between these three books. The exact nature of this relationship has been the subject of much debate. It seems that these three authors either read one another or some common source, which explains why so much of their substance and language are the same.

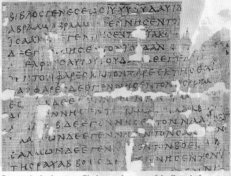

The Gospel of John, however, is different than the first three Gospels. John uses material that the other writers do not have. The wording of some of the stories is different. John often added details that the others do not include.

For example, the name of the woman who washed Jesus' feet with her hair (John 12:3) or that John beat Peter in a foot race to the empty tomb on Easter Sunday (John 20:4). Many of these details have a personal tone.

Papyrus 1, also known as P[1], shows a fragment of the Gospel of Matthew. The fragment, housed in the University of Pennsylvania Museum, dates to around AD 250.

The Synoptic Gospels Compared to John: Three Examples

THE GOSPEL TEXT	EVENT	DESCRIPTION
Matthew 3:11–12 Mark 1:7–8 Luke 3:15–18	John the Baptist's introduction of Jesus	General and generic language is used about the crowds.
John 1:24–44		John names specific individuals who become disciples of Jesus through John the Baptist.
Matthew 14:13–21 Mark 6:30–44 Luke 9:10–17	Feeding of the 5000	Dialogue with Jesus is attributed to the disciples as a group.
John 6:1–14		John names specific individuals who speak.
Matthew 28:1–10 Mark 16:1–11 Luke 24:1–12 John 20:1–18	The Resurrection	Individuals are named in all accounts to a greater or lesser extent. John is specific about the actions of Mary Magdalene, Peter and himself (the unnamed disciple).

The First Gospel

Because the first three Gospels so closely resemble each other, the question has long been asked, "Who wrote first?" Many modern scholars are inclined in favor of Mark as being the first Gospel in print. This is due in part to the brevity of the work and the fact that most of Mark's material can also be found in Matthew and Luke. The idea is that if Mark wrote first, Luke and Matthew might have read his work and added their own material in their writing. Early tradition holds that Mark became associated with Peter and that his Gospel might be a kind of "Memoirs of Peter." Its rapid-fire style seems like Peter's way of recounting Jesus' life.

Others are convinced, however, that none of the Gospels that exists today was the first to be in print. These scholars believe that there was an earlier writing that the authors of the present Gospels (Matthew, Mark and Luke) drew upon as a reference work. Papias, an early Christian and disciple of the Apostle John, wrote, "Matthew put together the sayings in the Hebrew language, and each one interpreted them as best he could" (in Eusebius, *Ecclesiastical History* 3.39.16). Since Matthew, was a tax collector (Matthew 9:9), he was a good pick to be the scribe among the disciples. So this tradition may bear some weight. It may be that Matthew recorded much of what happened in Jesus' ministry in the native tongue of Palestine. This document may later have been translated into Greek and used by him and the other synoptic writers to produce our present Gospels.

The Gospels as we now have them were first written in Greek, which was the popular common language of the Roman world. It is entirely possible that Matthew made the first record in Aramaic, but that Mark drafted the first Gospel in Greek drawing on Matthew's record and adding what he had heard from Peter. Luke and Matthew (in present form) would then have been written. John wrote his account after the others had been in circulation for some time.

Medieval manuscript known as *Aachen Gospels*, folio 13r, made around AD 820.

Harmonies Through History

Over the years, people have created different types of "Gospel Harmonies." These are some of the main types of harmonies:

- **Synthetic Harmonization:** One approach is to cut out any variation in similar accounts and replace it with preferred wording to create a kind of "official version."

- **Sequential Harmonization:** This type attempts to bring together two or more versions of an event by keeping both. The separate details are seen as separate incidents within the same story.

- **Parallel Harmonization:** A final approach may be to show two or more versions next to each other for comparison and contrast.

Gospel harmonies began to be produced early in the history of the church. Concern for accuracy and a full account of the gospel message became important for the church as it strove to remain faithful. These early harmonies bear witness to the church's use of the four canonical Gospels. Already by the post-apostolic age, the authority of the four to the exclusion of other texts is recognized.

AUTHOR	TITLE	DATE
Justin Martyr	Evident in his writings	Second Century
Tatian	Diatesseron	Second Century
Unknown	Dura-Europas Harmony	Second Century
Eusebius of Caesarea	Sections and Canons	Third Century
Augustine	Consensus of the Gospels	Fourth Century
Andreas Osiander	Gospel Harmony	Sixteenth Century

Contributing Authors: William Brent Ashby, BT; Benjamin Galan, MTS, ThM, Adjunct Professor of OT Hebrew and Literature at Fuller Seminary.

On page 33: Image of folio 27v with the symbols of the four Gospel writers, from *The Book of Kells*, around AD 800.

The Beatitudes

What Are the Beatitudes?
How Do They Relate to Us Today?

WHAT ARE THE BEATITUDES?

The word *beatitude* comes from a Latin word (*beatus*) that means "happy" or "blessed." So the word beatitude is about some happiness or blessedness. What does it mean to be happy or blessed? The answer to this question is found in the context of the Beatitudes in Matthew 5.

The Beatitudes are the first part of Jesus' teachings called the Sermon on the Mount, (Matthew 5:1–7:29). In Matthew 4:17 Jesus began his ministry by announcing the coming of the kingdom of heaven: "Repent, for the kingdom of heaven is near." In Matthew 4:23–25, Jesus healed the sick throughout Galilee. This healing was a demonstration of the coming kingdom of heaven, of the fulfillment of God's promises through his prophets in the Old Testament. The teachings in the Sermon on the Mount, then, are descriptions and instructions for those living in the kingdom of heaven.

The Beatitudes are not imperatives; they are not commands the believer must fulfill to enter the kingdom of God. Rather, they are results of the coming of this kingdom. They are part of the Gospel, the good news that Jesus, the Messiah, has come. The good news is that God was about to intervene decisively in history and produce people like the ones described in the Sermon on the Mount.

 ## Kingdom of God/Heaven

The expression "kingdom of heaven" only occurs in the Gospel according to Matthew. Why? Because the Gospel of Matthew appears to have been for a Jewish audience, Matthew avoids using the name of God—out of respect, Jews avoid pronouncing God's name.

- The idea of the kingdom uses an important metaphor in the Old Testament: God is King (Psalm 47:7). Kings in the ancient world had absolute power over their dominions. However, they also had responsibilities toward their subjects. Kings were supposed to:

    - *Provide protection for their territories and the people in them*
    - *Provide for the needs of their subjects*
    - *Maintain order in the kingdom, especially legal order*
    - *Represent the deity (in the Old Testament, God)—the king stood for God, representing his authority to the people*

BLESSED ARE THE POOR IN SPIRIT, FOR THEIRS IS THE KINGDOM OF HEAVEN.

MEANING

—Matthew 5:3

The "poor in spirit" are those who recognize their need for God in all things. Like the poor and destitute who depend on others, the poor in spirit know that only God can save and protect them.

What the WORLD Says	What JESUS Says
The world and every kind of human-made religion value the "spiritual master," the guru, the great teacher. The idea is that if you know and do the right things, you can find your own spiritual salvation. People have their own answers to their problems, if they could only recognize it.	Jesus tells us that the opposite is true. The truly happy people are those who have recognized they are spiritually bankrupt before God. Their happiness consists in relying on God's strength because they know he cannot fail, and having the certainty that in the kingdom of God, the Messiah will be fully in charge (Isaiah 29:19).

RELATED TEXTS

"Once more the humble will rejoice in the LORD..."
(Isaiah 29:19). See also: Luke 6:20; Matthew 18:4; Isaiah 61:1.

QUESTIONS

In what areas of your life are you trying to make it on your own, instead of asking God for help?

Now and Future Kingdom

- In the New Testament, the kingdom of heaven is God's gracious rule. In other words, it is where God's will is done. The gospels make it clear that the kingdom was a present experience (Luke 11:20, 17:21). Jesus' miracles, teachings, and ministry are all manifestations of the kingdom.

- Yet, the rest of the New Testament, the apostolic letters, makes it also clear that the kingdom is a reality in the future. That is, the fullness of the kingdom will only be experienced when Jesus comes back at the end of times.

- Some theologians call these two realities about the kingdom of heaven the "already-not yet." The kingdom of heaven and the promises within it are *already* part of the church's experience. However, the fullness of the kingdom's power and influence is *not yet* experienced. Christ will bring about the fullness of the kingdom in his second coming.

BLESSED ARE THOSE WHO MOURN, FOR THEY WILL BE COMFORTED.

—Matthew 5:4

MEANING

"Those who mourn" refers to people wishing God to send his Messiah, hoping God will restore his kingdom and set the world right. Isaiah 61:2–3 tells of the coming Messiah who will "comfort all who mourn, and provide for those who grieve in Zion". These are people who understand the mess the world is in and wish for God's redemption. Their comfort consists in knowing that the Messiah has come and the redemption they have hoped for is about to occur!

What the WORLD Says	What JESUS Says
Today we avoid grief and pain. "How can a mournful person be happy?" The pursuit of happiness has become for us a goal above all goals. We have become very adept to hiding from pain and reality. Nothing is solved, but we can continue to pretend to be happy.	In stark contrast, Jesus asserts that the way to true happiness must come through a radical shift in thought, a change of mind that first makes us see ourselves as we really are—and our world as it really is—and mourn. Only after we recognize this sorrow can God comfort us. Knowing that the Messiah has come and offers redemption is the greatest comfort for those who mourn.

RELATED TEXTS

"As a mother comforts her child, so will I comfort you..." (Isaiah 66:13).

"Do not let your hearts be troubled. Trust in God; trust also in me" (John 14:1).

"I tell you the truth, you will weep and mourn while the world rejoices. You will grieve, but your grief will turn to joy" (John 16:20).

"For the Lamb at the center of the throne will be their shepherd; he will lead them to springs of living water. And God will wipe away every tear from their eyes" (Revelation 7:17).

See also: Isaiah 61:2; John 16:7.

QUESTIONS

Ask God to show you things in your life to which you may be insensitive. Remember that the Lord will always be with you, comforting you through this painful process. If there are areas in your life that need changing, ask God to redeem them.

BLESSED ARE THE MEEK, FOR THEY WILL INHERIT THE EARTH.

—Matthew 5:5

MEANING

This beatitude alludes to Psalm 37:11: "But the meek will inherit the land...." The Psalm is comparing the "evil" and "wicked" with the meek. In fact, Psalm 37:3, 5 seem to define what the psalmist means by the meek, "Trust in the LORD and do good.... Commit your way to the LORD; trust in him...." The prophet Zephaniah uses the same expression during a prophetic oracle of judgment: "...because I will remove from this city those who rejoice in their pride... But I will leave within you the meek and humble, who trust in the name of the LORD" (Zephaniah 3:11–12).

In addition, the word *meek* is an important adjective in the Bible. It is used to describe Moses in Numbers 12:3, and usually translated as "humble." Jesus describes himself with the same word in Matthew 11:29, "...for I am gentle and humble in heart...." The third Beatitude, then, refers to the meekness necessary to trust in God. It also refers to the attitude of God's servant: the meekness to serve God and do his will above our own.

What the WORLD Says	What JESUS Says
It is the proud and strong who will inherit the earth. Only the mighty have the power to seize the prize of ruling the planet. Only those who are clever and confident in themselves and their abilities have any hope of holding on to authority and dominion. "Nice guys finish last" describes this attitude that gentleness never gets you anywhere.	Although it may appear that meekness is a disadvantage according to the values of this world, it is a wonderful thing in the values of God. It is God's invitation to trust in him, to have the certainty that his plans and work will accomplish what he promised.

Old Testament prophets communicated God's promise to restore the land to Israel. This promise was taken to be limited to the land that God originally promised to Abraham. But in the New Testament, the promise is extended. It is a promise for "a new heaven and a new earth" (Revelation 21:1, 2 Peter 3:13). It is the new heaven and new earth that the meek will inherit.

RELATED TEXTS

"For the Lord takes delight in his people; he crowns the humble with salvation" (Psalm 149:4).

See also: Psalm 37:3, 5, 11; 72:4; Isaiah 61:1; Numbers 12:3.

QUESTIONS

What areas of your life hinder you from obeying or accepting God's will? Pray that God will help you accept his will with meekness.

Old Testament Beatitudes

There are many beatitudes that occur in the Old Testament, some of which sound remarkably similar to Jesus' words.

- Psalm 41:1 says, "Blessed is he who has regard for the weak..." and we remember Jesus' beatitude about the merciful (Matthew 5:7).

- The book of Psalms opens with a blessing on righteous behavior: Jesus tells us that those who hunger and thirst for this righteousness shall be satisfied (Matthew 5:6).

- Psalm 32:1–2 presents a beatitude upon all whom the Lord has forgiven. The psalm goes on to speak of what it is like to confess utter dependence upon God. Jesus speaks of those who are poor in spirit as being blessed inheritors of the Kingdom of God.

- In Proverbs 8:34–35, personified wisdom says, "Blessed is the man who listens to me... for he who finds me finds life." Jesus ends the Sermon on the Mount by advising his hearers to take his words to heart. Then he reveals to them the consequences—it is a matter of life and death (Matthew 7:24–27).

BLESSED ARE THOSE WHO HUNGER AND THIRST FOR RIGHTEOUSNESS FOR THEY WILL BE FILLED.

—Matthew 5:6

MEANING

Just as poverty leads to hunger, the recognition of one's spiritual poverty leads to a hunger for righteousness. Jesus is talking to people who desire God's rule. It is a rule that brings justice for all. It is a reign in which God will satisfy the hungry and thirsty for righteousness. A fulfillment of God's promise in Isaiah 65:13, "My servants will eat...my servants will rejoice...."

What the WORLD Says	What JESUS Says
Hungering for things to be right is a fool's game. Nothing ever changes. It's fine to compromise and to set aside honor when doing what is right is inconvenient. It's all politics, so quit worrying about what is right, just go for what you need. You gotta look out for number one!	Jesus holds out the promise that those who are starved for righteousness will be satisfied. His kingdom is characterized by "righteousness, peace and joy in the Holy Spirit" (Romans 14:17).

RELATED TEXTS

"If anyone is thirsty, let him come to me and drink..." (John 7:37). See also: Isaiah 55:1–13; 65:13; John 6:48; Romans 14:17.

Blessings and Curses

Luke's gospel also contains a series of "woes" which are the opposites of the blessings (Luke 6:24–26).

- The woes describe the natural consequences to ignoring God's will. They tell us what we can expect if we do not live the way God desires.

- Here the blessings and curses are parallel, much the same as in Deuteronomy 28:1–19. At Mount Sinai, Moses set the covenant between God and the Israelites, laying out the natural consequences (both the blessings and the curses) of the people's responses.

- The parallel structure of the two passages gives the sermon in Luke's account the same authoritative feel of Moses' utterance. Jesus lays out its principles before his disciples and asks them the question, "Why do you call me, 'Lord, Lord,' and do not do what I say?" (Luke 6:46).

- It is clear Jesus claims authority for this teaching, and the Gospel of Matthew records the shock his hearers felt when faced with such claims (Matthew 7:28-29).

QUESTIONS

In what ways has God satisfied you when you have hungered and thirsted for righteousness?

BLESSED ARE THE MERCIFUL, FOR THEY WILL BE SHOWN MERCY.

—Matthew 5:7

MEANING

Mercy is part of God's own nature. "The LORD, the LORD, the compassionate and gracious God, slow to anger, abounding in love and faithfulness...." (Exodus 34:6). Besides, God expects mercy from his people: "He has shown you, O man, what is good. And what does the LORD require of you? To act justly and to love mercy and to walk humbly with your God" (Micah 6:8). People who have experienced mercy and forgiveness are filled with gratitude. Their gratitude cultivates a merciful attitude in return.

What the WORLD Says	What JESUS Says
"We want justice!" "Take no prisoners" are the slogans of the proud, the strong and the careless. We like to condemn others to make ourselves feel better. Our world idolizes the arrogant and merciless in the sports world, the world of wealth and fame, and on the movie screen. "We are the champions—no time for losers." Mercy has become a liability—it is way too costly and will prevent the attainment of our goals.	Jesus again challenges the way the rest of the world thinks. Jesus lifts up mercy as an essential quality. In fact, mercy is what Jesus' life was all about—God's mercy to us. In many places Jesus makes the connection between giving mercy and receiving it (See Matthew 6:12-15, 18:21-35). It is not that we can buy God's mercy by our own acts of mercy, but that only those who know God's mercy can be truly merciful and receive God's most precious gift—eternal life.

RELATED TEXTS

"But you, O Lord, are a compassionate and gracious God..." (Psalm 86:15).

"...Return to the LORD your God, for he is gracious and compassionate, slow to anger and abounding in love..." (Joel 2:13).

See also: Psalm 103:8, 145:8; Luke 6:36.

QUESTIONS

Which people in your life do you find it most difficult to be merciful to? In what practical ways can you demonstrate God's mercy in your local community?

BLESSED ARE THE PURE IN HEART FOR THEY WILL SEE GOD.

—Matthew 5:8

MEANING

Seeing God is one of the greatest hopes of the believer (1 John 3:2–3). But only the pure in heart may receive this blessing. Purity of heart, the heart that desires only what God wants, is not the result of personal effort. In other words, a pure heart is not the same as maturity of Christian experience. A pure heart is clean of sin. Only Christ can clean us from sin. God must give a pure heart (Psalm 51:10). Although purity of heart is not something we work towards, it is something we desire and God grants.

What the WORLD Says	What JESUS Says
While our culture values things like pure air, pure water, pure food, it seems to devalue the pure heart. Some people insist on a "smoke-free" environment but do not mind a polluted heart.	True happiness begins in the presence of God. It is a hope that sustains and inspires those living in the kingdom of heaven. One of Jesus' constant criticisms of the Jewish leaders was their hypocrisy. That is, their desire to appear pure and holy, while being corrupted and impure inside. Jesus came to fulfill the promise in Ezekiel 36:25–27: "I will sprinkle clean water on you, and you will be clean… I will give you a new heart and put a new spirit in you…."

RELATED TEXTS

"Create in me a pure heart, O God…" (Psalm 51:10).

"…But we know that when he appears, we shall be like him, for we shall see him as he is. Everyone who has this hope in him purifies himself, just as he is pure" (1 John 3:2–3).

See also: Exodus 33:20; Psalm 24:3–4; Psalm 51; Hebrews 12:14; Revelation 22:1–4.

QUESTIONS

What might happen if you pray to the Lord as David did in Psalm 51, verse 10: "Create in me a pure heart, O God, and renew a steadfast spirit within me"?

BLESSED ARE THE PEACEMAKERS FOR THEY WILL BE CALLED SONS OF GOD.

—Matthew 5:9

MEANING

This Beatitude brings together two important Old Testament concepts: peace and sons of God. Peace is a central characteristic of the kingdom of heaven. "The wolf will live with the lamb, the leopard will lie down with the goat, the calf and the lion and the yearling together, and a little child will lead them..." (Isaiah 11:6). Those who would normally be at war with each other will be in harmony. All things are made right and peace prevails. The Old Testament applies the title of "son of God" to the Messiah (Psalm 2:7). However, in the New Testament, the Apostle Paul explains that when we are in Christ, we "receive the full rights of sons;" in other words, we are made adopted children of God (Galatians 4:5).

What the WORLD Says	What JESUS Says
Peace at any price, Give peace a chance. Peace—the cessation of all conflict—has become what a world in war is desperately looking for. Some feel world peace would solve all problems; others are ready to buy peace at almost any cost. Many seek a personal peace through a variety of avenues—drugs, music, meditation, and others. Still, the cessation of conflict will not substitute for true peace, the kind of peace Jesus offers.	Jesus, before leaving this earth, promised his disciples his peace: "Peace I leave with you; my peace I give you. I do not give to you as the world gives..." (John 14:27). His peace is a clear sign that the kingdom is in our midst. Only Jesus makes this peace possible (Ephesians 2:14) and only in him we become adopted children (Galatians 4:5).

RELATED TEXTS

"If it is possible, as far as it depends on you, live at peace with everyone" (Romans 12:18).

See also: Psalm 4:8; Isaiah 9:6; Romans 5:1.

QUESTIONS

Can you think of a difficult or painful time in your life when you experienced Jesus' peace in a special way? How is the peace that Jesus gives different from the kind of peace the world promises?

BLESSED ARE THOSE WHO ARE PERSECUTED BECAUSE OF RIGHTEOUSNESS, FOR THEIRS IS THE KINGDOM OF HEAVEN.

—Matthew 5:10

MEANING

Just like the kingdom of heaven belongs to the poor in spirit, it also belongs to the ones persecuted because of righteousness. This verse is a reminder of God's prophets in the Old Testament. These were people who stood in for the right. They encountered opposition; they were mocked and harmed because they stood for what was right. But their reward is great. They truly enjoy the benefits of the kingdom of heaven.

What the WORLD Says	What JESUS Says
Principles are good, but not if they get you killed or cause you grief. Righteousness has little foundation in our world today. Standards for right and wrong are not defined by what God desires for our good. People get away with what they can.	Jesus made it clear to his disciples that persecution would occur: "If they persecuted me, they will persecute you also" (John 15:20). Often doing what is right leads people to feel lonely, isolated, and persecuted. However, Jesus promised that he would not leave these people alone. He sent the Holy Spirit to guide and comfort. Besides, he also promises that "Now is your time of grief, but I will see you again and you will rejoice, and no one will take away your joy" (John 16:22).

RELATED TEXTS

"And the God of all grace, who called you to his eternal glory in Christ, after you have suffered a little while, will himself restore you and make you strong, firm and steadfast" (1 Peter 5:10).

"But even if you should suffer for what is right, you are blessed... But in your hearts set apart Christ as Lord..." (1 Peter 3:14–15).

See also: Luke 6:22–23; John 15:18–21.

QUESTIONS

Think of a time when you felt like speaking up for what was right. If you did not speak up, what prevented you from doing so? If you did, what resulted from it? How can you help others who are facing persecution because of righteousness?

BLESSED ARE THOSE WHO HAVE NOT SEEN YET HAVE BELIEVED.

—John 20:29

MEANING

Jesus is speaking about his resurrection. It is one thing to have seen the risen Christ as hundreds of his disciples did (1 Corinthians 15:6) and yet another to believe today based on the word of these eyewitnesses. There is a special blessing experienced by those who know that Christ has risen, based on the testimony alone.

What the WORLD Says	What JESUS Says
"Who really knows what happened back there 2000 years ago?" "People don't just get up from the dead. The whole thing was probably a hoax or a mistake." There is much skepticism about the events that eyewitness recorded in the Bible.	"I am the resurrection and the life" (John 11:25). We have the testimony of the Apostles (1 Corinthians 15:3-8), and the ministry of the Holy Spirit (John 15:26).

RELATED TEXTS

"Though you have not seen him, you love him; and even though you do not see him now, you believe in him and are filled with an inexpressible and glorious joy…" (1 Peter 1:8).

See also: John 1:12, 17:20–21; 1 Corinthians 15.

QUESTIONS

When have you seen God give the gift of faith to yourself or other believers?

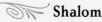 **Shalom**

Traditionally, this Hebrew word is translated as "peace." When we think about peace, we tend to define it as absence of conflict. However, *shalom* means much more than that.

- The best example of what *shalom* means is the Garden of Eden. In Eden, all things functioned according to the order and purpose that God assigned them. There was order and harmony, balance and wholeness.
- When Adam and Eve rebelled against God, this state of being was broken. Things are no longer the way they are supposed to be.

IT IS MORE BLESSED TO GIVE THAN TO RECEIVE.

MEANING

—Acts 20:35

Giving, especially to those who are in need, will lead to happiness quicker than if we are only on the receiving end. The life that constantly takes without giving is a selfish life, and selfishness only leads to greater unhappiness. Meeting other peoples' needs is the road to a blessed life.

What the WORLD Says	What JESUS Says
"Get what you can now—after all, the one who dies with the most toys wins." No one's going to take care of you. If you're generous, you'll be taken advantage of. You have to make it on your own. Besides, you can't please everyone, so you have to please yourself. Charity is a scam, so get what you can, and take what you can get.	Jesus tells us that he came to serve, not to be served (Matthew 20:28). He came to give himself and calls us to the same lifestyle. It is easy to miss that this giving was a joy to him because he delighted to do what God had called him to (John 17:13). "A servant is not greater than his master" and we are blessed when we follow the Master's example (John 13:15–17).

RELATED TEXTS

"…And if you spend yourselves in behalf of the hungry and satisfy the needs of the oppressed, then your light will rise in the darkness, and your night will become like the noonday" (Isaiah 58:10). See also: Matthew 6:1–4; Luke 6:38; 22:24–30.

- *Shalom* is about relationships. When humans sinned in the Garden, three relationships were broken:
    1. *Our relationship with God;*
    2. *Our relationship with Creation;*
    3. *Our relationship with each other.*
- Jesus brings peace in all these relationships. Jesus restores this *shalom*.
- The kingdom of heaven is the context in which *shalom* prevails. Things work according to God's original design. Only in this context, true joy is possible.

QUESTIONS

When have you experienced giving as a delight? When has it not been a joy? Ask God to help you release your grip on worldly riches, so that you can have a servant's heart like Jesus.

Righteousness

- Righteousness in the Old Testament was a relational concept.

  It described a legal relationship. That is, it was a relationship in terms of law, courts, judges, and so on (see Psalm 9:4; Psalm 15; Isaiah 5:7). In other words, it meant ethical or fair behavior.

  It described a covenant relationship. It is a description of God's relating and doing right toward his people; it was also the expected behavior of God's people toward God (see, Ezekiel 18:5–9, 25–32).

- Righteousness in the New Testament reflected the two-fold distinction in the Old Testament.

  The Apostle Paul expanded the legal sense of the concept. He applied it to Christ's work. Because of Jesus' atoning death on the cross (he died in our place), God makes right (justifies) sinners (Romans 4:5). Paul did not mean that God makes people righteous—that we can now only do what is right. Rather, he meant that God has applied Christ's righteousness—his perfect obedience and guiltlessness—to us, so we become "legally" (in the sense of a court proceeding) acquitted of the penalty of sin, which is death.

  In Matthew, Jesus was not using the "legal" sense of the concept. Rather, righteousness in the Sermon on the Mount goes back to the "covenant relationship" sense. That is, in the kingdom of heaven, relationships are restored: (1) relationship between God and humanity; (2) relationship between humanity and creation; and (3) relationships among humans. In the kingdom of heaven, people relate rightly, doing what is right in all relationships.

Contributing Authors: William Brent Ashby, BT; Benjamin Galan, MTS, ThM

The Lord's Prayer

Know God's Power & Forgiveness
Through the Seven Petitions

Lord, Teach Us to Pray

Jesus' disciples had seen him pray many times. Sometimes he prayed all night and sometimes his prayers were just one sentence. But Jesus' followers made the connection between Jesus' intense prayer life and the power he showed in every aspect of life. They must have realized that prayer was the link. Finally, one disciple asked Jesus to teach them how to pray. Jesus gave them a deceptively simple, childlike prayer which has come to be known as "The Lord's Prayer." The prayer is recorded in Luke 11:2-4 and Matthew 6:9-13. Matthew's version highlights seven key parts:

> *Our Father in heaven,*
> *hallowed be your name,*
> *your kingdom come,*
> *your will be done on earth as it is in heaven.*
> *Give us today our daily bread.*
> *Forgive us our debts, as we also have forgiven our debtors.*
> *And lead us not into temptation, but deliver us from the evil one.*
>
> —Matthew 6:9-13

In this pattern, Jesus provided his followers with guidelines for prayer based on the attributes or characteristics of God.

The two main sections of the prayer divide with the words "your" and "our."

1. The first part centers on God, putting God in his rightful place in our priorities. Only by focusing on the patient and loving Father can we find the attitude that puts our own needs in perspective.

2. The second part focuses on our needs—body, soul, and spirit—and the needs of others. In just three brief requests, Jesus targets all of human behavior and character and reminds us that we always need him. It's been said that if these three requests are prayed properly, nothing more need be said. Only in moment-by-moment dependence on God will we experience the good things God wants to provide.

The Lord's Prayer is a dangerous, life-changing prayer. Jesus' enemies eventually killed him for asserting his close tie to God through addressing God as "Father." Until Jesus gave his followers the right to be called children of God, this would have been blasphemy.

Twenty-first century Christians may take the privilege for granted, but the prayer is still a dangerous one: We do, in one sense, "take our lives in our hands" and offer them up again and again as sacrifice to the One who gave us all in the first place, receiving all of Life in return.

GOD'S ATTRIBUTE

WHAT DOES IT MEAN?

SCRIPTURE

APPLICATION

*O*ur Father in heaven (NIV)
*O*ur Father which art in heaven (KJV)

GOD'S FATHERLY LOVE

God is a loving and compassionate Father who gives life, provides for and protects those who trust him. Like a caring human father, God wants a close relationship with his children. Addressing God as "Our Father" plunges the person praying into a relationship. A child approaching a loving father knows that father will give careful attention to the child's requests and will be lovingly inclined toward the child's best interests. The child knows the father will answer. This is how Jesus tells us to approach God—as trusting children of a patient, tender father.

But to all who believed him [Jesus] and accepted him, he gave the right to become children of God. They are reborn—not with a physical birth resulting from human passion or plan, but a birth that comes from God.
—John 1:12, 13 (New Living Translation)

How great is the love the Father has lavished on us, that we should be called children of God! —1 John 3:1

Let us then approach the throne of grace with confidence, so that we may receive mercy and find grace to help us in our time of need.
—Hebrews 4:16

During Jesus' time, people understood God to be awesome, majestic, and far away in the unreachable heavens. Though the Old Testament uses the metaphor of fatherhood when talking of God, no one would have dreamed of addressing God as "Father" in prayer. Jesus' use of the name "Abba" (like our "Daddy") must have stunned his disciples. In fact, Jesus' use of the family name was so shocking to the religious leaders of his day that eventually he was accused of blasphemy and crucified for identifying himself as God's Son!

Jesus taught his followers that they should address God as "Father," and that their loving Father would care for all the needs of those who trust in him (see Matthew 7:7-11). Then, not only did Jesus encourage that relationship of trust, but he willingly died a horrible death to purchase the right of believers in Christ to be called children of God! It's hard to comprehend that the God who has all the power in the universe will listen to our prayers because of the actions of his Son, Jesus!

*H*allowed be your name (NIV)
*H*allowed be thy name (KJV)

GOD'S HOLINESS

To hallow means to make holy. To "hallow" God's name means to honor it as holy and sacred. When we pray, we enter the presence of God with reverence, worship, and thanksgiving. We thank God not only for what he's done, but also for who he is. God's greatness and glory alone are worthy of praise and thankfulness. Thanksgiving recognizes that everything we have belongs to God, whether it be our talents, possessions, jobs, or children.

Exalt the LORD our God and worship at his holy mountain, for the LORD our God is holy. —Psalm 99:9

You shall not misuse the name of the LORD your God, for the LORD will not hold anyone guiltless who misuses his name. —Exodus 20:7

So whether you eat or drink or whatever you do, do it all for the glory of God. —1 Corinthians 10:31

The earth is the Lord's, and everything in it, the world, and all who live in it. —Psalm 24:1

Traditionally, God's people, the Jews, never said or wrote the name of God. To do so was considered not keeping the name of God holy. God's name represents his character, his plan, and his will. We often think of cursing as a common misuse of God's name, but what about attitudes of the heart? Lack of respect or indifference by one who professes love for God may be just as much a sin. Revelations 3:15, 16 shows God's attitude toward indifference: "I know your deeds, that you are neither cold nor hot. I wish you were either one or the other! So, because you are lukewarm—neither hot nor cold—I am about to spit you out of my mouth."

Jesus encouraged his followers to use God's name in honorable ways and for purposes that deepen and endear our bonds to him. Part of showing reverence for the holy name of God is thanking him for who he is and for what he's done. Many Psalms praise and worship God's holy name (see Psalms 100 and 148). Our greatest reverence, though, is shown by the stories our lives reveal. Our Father's name is most hallowed when we live in ways that attract others to him. (See 1 Corinthians 10:31; Matthew 5:16.)

Your kingdom come (NIV)
Thy kingdom come (KJV)

GOD'S SOVEREIGNTY

God has supreme power and authority over everything in heaven and earth. When we acknowledge God's sovereignty, we affirm and welcome his reign in our lives. We promise to live in ways that honor him. But God's kingdom is both here and now—and yet to come. During Jesus' life on earth, his ministry was "to proclaim freedom for the prisoners, to recover sight for the blind, to release the oppressed, and to proclaim the year of the Lord's favor" (Luke 4:18, 19). When Jesus was around, people were freed from sickness, suffering, and pain. When Jesus returns to reign supreme, there will be no pain, suffering, or evil ever again. God will make everything right in the end.

In the time of those kings, the God of heaven will set up a kingdom that will never be destroyed, nor will it be left to another people. It will crush all those kingdoms and bring them to an end, but it will itself endure forever.—Daniel 2:44

And I heard a loud voice from the throne saying, "Now the dwelling of God is with men, and he will live with them. They will be his people, and God himself will be with them and be their God. He will wipe every tear from their eyes. There will be no more death or mourning or crying or pain, for the old order of things has passed away."
—Revelation 21:3, 4

Jesus said that the Kingdom of God was near (Mark 1:15). When asked when the Kingdom of God would come, Jesus said, "The kingdom of God does not come with your careful observation, nor will people say, 'Here it is,' or 'There it is,' because the kingdom of God is within you." God's kingdom will be evident in the lives of those who make him their Lord. This petition asks the Lord to change our lives so that his goodness is always evident through us. Some people have interpreted this prayer as an invitation to impact culture by passing laws calling people back to safer moral standards. But Jesus made clear his Church's mission: to lead people to himself. Jesus commissioned all disciples to proclaim that Jesus is King and Lord over all (Matthew 28:18-20). Our obedience to this commission helps spread God's kingdom throughout the world. This prayer can function as a petition for the strength and power we need to usher in God's kingdom on earth. When we focus on recognizing and embracing God's reign in this world, we help to make it visible.

Your will be done on earth as it is in heaven (NIV)
Thy will be done in earth, as it is in heaven (KJV)

GOD'S AUTHORITY

God's perfect will is always being done in heaven. But on earth, human free will results in selfishness, greed, and evil. In this part of the Lord's Prayer, we ask that God's will would take place on earth. More specifically, we pray for God's will to become our will.

God calls each one of his children to live rightly and do good to others, caring for those around us as much as for ourselves. We pray that all people submit to the will of God over their own desires and faithfully love God and neighbors as themselves. Relationship with God depends on obedience to his will. God's will should be the context for everything we ask for, say, and do.

Teach me to do your will, for you are my God;
may your good Spirit lead me on level ground. —Psalm 143:10

Not everyone who says to me, "Lord, Lord," will enter the kingdom of heaven,
but only he who does the will of my Father who is in heaven.
—Matthew 7:21

Jesus prayed for his Father's will: "Yet not as I will, but as you will." —Matthew 26:39

For whoever does the will of my Father in heaven is my brother and sister and mother.
—Matthew 12:50

Philippians 2:3-8 says, "Do nothing out of selfish ambition or vain conceit, but in humility consider others better than yourselves." Our attitude should be like Jesus'. So often, when we come to God in prayer, we bring our own agendas. We want our will to be done, we want our wishes to be granted, and we want God to answer our prayers in a certain way. Often God's will differs from our own; in these situations, we need to trust God's will over our own desires.

For centuries, Christians have debated whether God's will is done whether or not we pray. Some question, "Why pray if God knows everything we need before we ask?"

Others have wondered whether God takes action at all if we don't initiate the request. While we trust in God's sovereignty and his ability to exercise his good will, we also trust his commands to exercise the muscles of our wills in prayer. We pray, believing in God's promises to respond in ways that are best for us (see Luke 18:1). Though we often pray for changes in circumstance, the real work of prayer changes us from the inside out (Romans 12:1, 2). The more we talk with God, the more we find ourselves wanting to please him. Prayer often changes our circumstances, but more importantly, it changes us and our priorities.

*G*ive us this day our daily bread (NIV)
*G*ive us this day our daily bread (KJV)

GOD'S PROVIDENCE

God is able to provide for all our needs. The Greek word for "bread" represents not just food, but every physical thing we need. When we pray for our daily bread, we ask God to provide for our material, physical, emotional, relational, and spiritual needs for that day. Daily bread can include the daily needs of ministries, people, communities, leaders, family, friends, as well as personal needs. God commits himself to provide for his children, yet God knows more about what we need than we ourselves know. By praying for daily bread, we are not taking it for granted, but acknowledging that all our life depends on his mercy.

But seek first his kingdom and his righteousness, and all these things will be given to you as well. Therefore do not worry about tomorrow, for tomorrow will worry about itself. Each day has enough trouble of its own. —Matthew 6:33, 34

Then Jesus declared, "I am the bread of life. He who comes to me will never go hungry, and he who believes in me will never be thirsty." —John 6:35

Every good and perfect gift is from above, coming down from the Father of the heavenly lights, who does not change like shifting shadows. —James 1:17

The phrase "this day" shows that we rely on God one day at a time. Compared to the rest of people on earth, we are wealthy Christians. It's far too easy for us to forget that not only our talents, resources, and opportunities come from God, but also the next meal. Asking for what we need each day— even if it's already in our refrigerators—encourages a relationship with the One who gives all. He wants us to remember and ask for his help with the most basic needs: disciplining our children, speaking to a spouse, growing spiritually, resolving a conflict with a friend, reuniting with family members, leading ministries, conducting an office meeting, and going to the movies.

So what if we ask for the wrong things—things that, while they may be good in themselves are not in God's plan for us? As a loving Father, God will always give us what's best for us, not necessarily what we want. What we receive will be what's right for us and fits God's greater goal of transforming us to be more like him.

*F*orgive us our debts,
as we also have forgiven our debtors (NIV)
*A*nd forgive us our debts, as we forgive our debtors (KJV)

GOD'S MERCY

We ask God to forgive the wrong we have done as well as our neglect of the good things we should have done. But there is a catch: God will forgive us only as much as we forgive those who have injured us. God is merciful and he expects us to be also. If we refuse to forgive others, how can we expect God's forgiveness?

Debts vs. Trespasses

Several Greek words are used to describe sin. The Lord's prayer in the Gospel of Matthew uses the word *ophelema* which is rendered "debt" (Matthew 6:12). However, only two verses later, the gospel uses the word *paraptoma*, which is usually rendered "trespass" (Matthew 6:14). In all these cases, sin is what separates us from God, our friends, and our family. Without forgiveness—whether it be forgiving debts or forgiving trespasses—relationships suffer and redemption is not possible.

If we confess our sins, he is faithful and just and will forgive us our sins and purify us from all unrighteousness. —1 John 1:9

For as high as the heavens are above the earth, so great is his love for those who fear him; as far as the east is from the west, so far has he removed our transgressions from us. —Psalm 103:12, 13

No longer will a man teach his neighbor, or a man his brother, saying, "Know the Lord," because they will all know me, from the least of them to the greatest. For I will forgive their wickedness and will remember their sins no more. —Hebrews 8:11, 12

The New Testament uses five Greek words to talk about sin. The meanings range from slipping and falling (unintentional), "missing the mark" as an arrow misses the target, stepping across the line (intentional), "lawlessness" or open rebellion against God, and the word used in Matthew 6:12, which refers to a spiritual debt to God. This last aspect of sin is what Jesus illustrates in the following story:

Jesus told a parable about a man who owed the king over one million dollars. After the man begged for mercy, the king forgave the debt. Afterward, that same man demanded a few dollars from his neighbor. When his neighbor could not pay, the man had him thrown into prison. Once the king heard about it, he had the man turned over to the jailers until he could repay the debt. Jesus finished by saying, "This is how my heavenly Father will treat each of you unless you forgive your brother from your heart" (Matthew 18:23-35). Jesus makes it clear that God will not show mercy to the merciless!

Sometimes we are unaware of our sins. Therefore, praying for forgiveness requires listening quietly in God's presence so that he may reveal to us our own acts of disobedience, our resentments, and our unresolved issues.

*A*nd lead us not into temptation,
but deliver us from the evil one (NIV)
*A*nd lead us not into temptation, but deliver us from evil (KJV)

GOD'S PROTECTION

We are taught to pray that we won't be tempted to do wrong. In a practical way, this is like praying that God will keep our minds off of tempting situations. People used to excuse bad behavior by saying, "The devil made me do it." But in reality, the devil cannot make us do wrong. We do it ourselves. God won't make us obey him, but he does give us the power to walk away from wrong choices. The Holy Spirit gives us strength to withstand temptation, avoid sin, and strive for holiness. Satan is constantly seeking to attack the hearts and minds of those who love God. God provides us with the defenses we need to protect ourselves against the weapons of Satan. By praying for protection, we prepare each day for battle against evil.

No temptation has seized you except what is common to man. And God is faithful; he will not let you be tempted beyond what you can bear. But when you are tempted, he will also provide a way out so that you can stand up under it. —1 Corinthians 10:13

Therefore put on the full armor of God, so that when the day of evil comes, you may be able to stand your ground. —Ephesians 6:10-13a

In this you greatly rejoice, though now for a little while you may have had to suffer grief in all kinds of trials. These have come so that your faith—of greater worth than gold, which perishes even though refined by fire—may be proved genuine and may result in praise, glory and honor when Jesus Christ is revealed. —1 Peter 1:6, 7

The Greek word for "temptation" emphasizes the idea of testing or proving, rather than simply an enticement to sin. The Bible is clear that God is good and holy, and he would never lead us into sin. James 1:13, 14 says that God does not tempt anyone, but each person is tempted by his own evil desire. So why do we pray this petition? Because it's better to avoid danger and all the trouble caused by sin than to have to fight and face the possibility of losing to it! Realistically, having the potential to do evil is part of being a human being—it gives us the opportunity to show what we are becoming. Genuine freedom requires that there be a choice between good and evil.

Yet, we also know that trials strengthen faith and character (1 Peter 1:6, 7). Through our trials, we are driven closer to God through prayer and Scripture. We are reminded not to place our trust in ourselves. Through trials, we learn to trust God more, and we gain the ability to help others in similar trials. So while human nature resists the realities of trials and temptations, the maturing Christian accepts the refining process they bring. All that's left is to throw ourselves on the Father who has promised not to leave us unprotected and exposed to attacks from the enemy (Satan), but to protect, deliver, and forgive.

REASONS TO FORGIVE

Reason	Result	Bible Passage
Forgiveness is characteristic of a Christian life.	By loving our enemies, we show that we are children of God.	Blessed are the merciful, for they will be shown mercy. —Matthew 5:7
	When a Christian refuses to forgive, that person puts himself above God as judge.	You have heard that it was said, "Love your neighbor and hate your enemy." But I tell you: Love your enemies and pray for those who persecute you, that you may be sons of your Father in heaven. He causes his sun to rise on the evil and the good, and sends rain on the righteous and the unrighteous. —Matthew 5:43-45
We follow Jesus, our role model, who forgave.	Only through Jesus are we forgiven and made right with God.	Be kind and compassionate to one another, forgiving each other, just as in Christ God forgave you. —Ephesians 4:32
	Whatever we may suffer cannot come close to the offenses Jesus Christ forgave during his time on earth.	Whoever claims to live in him must walk as Jesus did. —1 John 2:6 Jesus said, "Father, forgive them, for they do not know what they are doing." —Luke 23:34
We are made in the image of God, who forgives.	We reflect the beauty and glory of our Creator when we forgive.	A man's wisdom gives him patience; it is to his glory to overlook an offense. —Proverbs 19:11
Forgiveness keeps Satan from gaining a foothold.	Forgiveness frees the conscience of guilt and brings peace of mind.	If you forgive anyone, I also forgive him. And what I have forgiven— if there was anything to forgive— I have forgiven in the sight of Christ for your sake, in order that Satan might not outwit us. For we are not unaware of his schemes. —2 Corinthians 2:10, 11
Christ's Body, the Church, cannot function without forgiveness.	Grudges and resentments tarnish the Church's witness and prevent the full benefits of God's gifts.	Therefore, if you are offering your gift at the altar and there remember that your brother has something against you, leave your gift there in front of the altar. First go and be reconciled to your brother; then come and offer your gift. —Matthew 5:23, 24
Only by forgiving others can we expect our own prayers for forgiveness to be answered.	God will treat us in the same way we treat others.	For if you forgive men when they sin against you, your heavenly Father will also forgive you. But if you do not forgive men their sins, your Father will not forgive your sins. —Matthew 6:14, 15

OTHER VERSES ON PRAYER

Abide in Christ

If you remain in me and my words remain in you, ask whatever you wish, and it will be given you. —John 15:7

Ask, Seek and Knock

Ask and it will be given to you; seek and you will find; knock and the door will be opened to you. For everyone who asks receives; he who seeks finds; and to him who knocks, the door will be opened. —Matthew 7:7, 8

Do Not Be Anxious

Do not be anxious about anything, but in everything, by prayer and petition, with thanksgiving, present your requests to God. And the peace of God, which transcends all understanding, will guard your hearts and your minds in Christ Jesus. —Philippians 4:6, 7

Pray Continually

Be joyful always; pray continually; give thanks in all circumstances, for this is God's will for you in Christ Jesus. —1 Thessalonians 5:16-18

God Knows What We Need

In the same way, the Spirit helps us in our weakness. We do not know what we ought to pray for, but the Spirit himself intercedes for us with groans that words cannot express. And he who searches our hearts knows the mind of the Spirit, because the Spirit intercedes for the saints in accordance with God's will. —Romans 8:26, 27

Prayer Is Effective

Is any one of you in trouble? He should pray. Is anyone happy? Let him sing songs of praise. Is any one of you sick? He should call the elders of the church to pray over him and anoint him with oil in the name of the Lord. And the prayer offered in faith will make the sick person well; the Lord will raise him up. If he has sinned, he will be forgiven. Therefore confess your sins to each other and pray for each other so that you may be healed. The prayer of a righteous man is powerful and effective. —James 5:13-16

HOW CAN I PRAY?

How can I pray **"our"** if I live only for myself?

How can I pray **"Father"** if I do not act like his child?

How can I pray **"who art in heaven"** if I am laying up no treasure there?

How can I pray **"hallowed be Thy name"** if I don't care about being holy myself?

How can I pray **"Thy kingdom come"** if I live for *my* kingdom, power, and wealth?

How can I pray **"Thy will by done"** if I disobey his Word?

How can I pray **"on earth as it is in heaven"** if I will not serve him here and now?

How can I pray **"give us … our daily bread"** if I am dishonest or unwilling to share what I have with others?

How can I pray **"forgive us our debts"** if I nurture resentment against another?

How can I pray **"lead us not into temptation"** if I willingly place myself in its path?

How can I pray **"deliver us from evil"** if I refuse to put on all of God's armor?

How can I pray **"Thine is the kingdom"** if my life does not reflect his lordship?

How can I pray **"Thine is the … power"** if I fear what people may do?

How can I pray **"Thine is the … glory"** if I seek honor for myself?

How can I pray **"forever"** if my life is bounded only by the things of time?

THE LORD'S PRAYER

Rather than giving us a formula to repeat over and over, Jesus gave us a model prayer illustrating first of all what our relationship with God should be like (the total dependence of children on a loving Father), and also the three main purposes of prayer:

- To declare God's holiness
- To usher in God's kingdom
- To do God's will

Seven distinct parts emphasize seven of God's attributes that help to place all of our needs and desires in proper perspective.

GOD'S ATTRIBUTE	FOCUS	PETITION
God's Love	God is a loving Father	Our Father in heaven
God's Holiness	God's name is holy	Hallowed be your name
God's Sovereignty	There is no one above God	Your kingdom come
God's Authority	God has the supreme authority	Your will be done on earth as it is in heaven
God's Providence	God is the source of everything we need	Give us today our daily bread
God's Mercy	Forgiveness is our greatest need	Forgive us our debts, as we also have forgiven our debtors
God's Protection	Trials prove our faith and develop our characters	And lead us not into temptation, but deliver us from the evil one

Contributor: Shawn Vander Lugt, M.Div.

CHAPTER 6

Names
of Jesus

50 Names of Jesus

The Meaning of Each Name

Bible References

Name	References	Meaning
ALMIGHTY	Revelation 1:8	Jesus is all-powerful.
AUTHOR AND FINISHER	Hebrews 12:2	Jesus is our start and finish.
BELOVED	Ephesians 1:6	Jesus is at the center of God's love.
BRANCH	Isaiah 11:1; Jeremiah 23:5; Zechariah 3:8; 6:12	Jesus is the shoot from David's line.
BREAD OF LIFE	John 6:32-35	Jesus is our sustenance.
BRIDEGROOM	Matthew 9:15; John 3:29; Rev. 21:9	Jesus leads and cares for us.
BRIGHT MORNING STAR	Revelation 22:16	Jesus lights our way.
CARPENTER	Mark 6:3	Jesus is one of us.
CHOSEN ONE	Luke 23:35	Jesus is God's Chosen One.
CHIEF CORNERSTONE	Isaiah 28:16; Psalm 118:22; Ephesians 2:20; 1 Peter 2:6	Jesus is our rock of safety.
DOOR	John 10:9	Jesus is our gateway.
EMMANUEL/ IMMANUEL	Isaiah 7:14 – 8:8; Matthew 1:23	Jesus is God with us.

Insights	Related Titles (by root word and/or theme)
Christ is the All-Powerful Lord. Nothing is beyond His reach or impossible for Him.	Mighty God, Mighty in Battle, Potentate, Power of God (Isaiah 9:6; Psalm 24:8; 1 Timothy 6:15; 1 Corinthians 1:24)
Jesus was at the beginning of creation and will be there to the end. He is both the author of all that is and the one who sees His creation through to the end.	Alpha and Omega, Beginning and End, First and Last (Revelation 1:8; 21:6; 22:13)
Christ is the Beloved Son of the Father, and as such, the desire of all people who love God. All who love God will be drawn to Jesus.	Desire of all nations (Haggai 2:7) Associate of God (Zechariah 13:7)
Jesus is the offshoot of the line of David and paradoxically also the root. He is the vine on which we depend for life and nourishment.	Nazarene (Netzer = Branch in Hebrew; Matthew 2:23; Isaiah 11:1) Root of David, Shoot, Vine (Revelation 5:5; Isaiah 11:10; 53:2; John 15:1)
Jesus was born in Bethlehem, which means "the house of bread." He is our spiritual nourishment and the sustenance of the world. All things are kept alive by Him.	Living Bread (John 6:5) Living Water (John 7:37, 38)
Jesus is the bridegroom and His church is the bride. He is the head of the church and cares for her.	Head of the Church (Ephesians 5:23) Head of the Body (Ephesians 4:15, 16)
Jesus is the brightest star in the heavens and the Light of the World. We shall not lose our way in His light.	Day Star (2 Peter 1:19) Star (Numbers 24:17) Sunrise (Luke 1:78) Sun of Righteousness (Malachi 4:2)
Jesus, the creator of wood, became a worker of wood, and died on a cross of wood for us (Galatians 3:13).	Carpenter's Son (Matthew 13:55)
Jesus is God's Chosen One, chosen for glory and great sacrifice. We, in Him, are God's chosen people.	Elect One (Isaiah 42:1)
Jesus is the cornerstone which the religious leaders rejected, but which God chose from eternity to build His house, a temple of living stone! We can rely on Him as our solid foundation.	Foundation, Living Stone, Precious Stone, Rock, Rock of Offense, Stone (1 Corinthians 3:11; 1 Peter 2:4; Isaiah 28:16; 1 Corinthians 10:4; 1 Peter 2:8; Psalm 118:22)
Jesus is our opening to God. He is the only way to heaven.	Door of the Sheepfold (John 10:7) See *Way*.
Jesus was born on earth as a real human being. He entered space and time to become one of us so we might be with God forever.	Only Begotten God (John 1:18)

Name	References	Meaning
ETERNAL FATHER	Isaiah 9:6; 1 John 1:1-3	Jesus is forever.
FAITHFUL AND TRUE WITNESS	Revelation 1:5; 3:14	Jesus is faithful.
FIRSTBORN	Hebrews 12:23; Revelation 5	Jesus is our elder brother.
GOD	John 1:1, 14-18; Romans 9:5; Titus 2:13; Heb. 1:8	Jesus is God.
HEAD OF THE CHURCH	Ephesians 5:23	Jesus leads the church.
HIGH PRIEST, APOSTLE	Hebrews 3:1, 2	Jesus is our prophet and priest.
HOLY ONE	Mark 1:24; Acts 2:27; 3:14; Psalm 16:10	Jesus is perfect.
HOPE	1 Timothy 1:1	Jesus is our confidence.
IMAGE OF THE INVISIBLE GOD	2 Corinthians 4:4; Colossians 1:15	Jesus is the perfect picture of God.
JESUS	Matthew 1:21	Jesus saves.
JUDGE/RULER	John 5:22, 23; Micah 4:3; Matthew 26:67; Acts 10:42	Jesus is our judge as well as our advocate and lawyer.

Insights

Christ had no beginning and has no end. He is the source of time, space, and all creation.

Christ is Truth in the flesh. His witness is always faithful. We can trust His word.

Christ is the firstborn of the dead, the firstfruits of a new humanity, resurrected in new form. As our eldest brother (Hebrews 2:11), He is heir of all things. (The importance of the firstborn is also connected to Passover. At the Exodus, the firstborn child of the Hebrews was "passed over." He was saved from death by the sacrifice of a lamb.)

Christ is in His very nature God and all the fullness of that essence is in Him. He is worthy of our worship.

Jesus is the leader and Lord of the church. True believers will follow Him as He cares for them and directs their way.

An apostle is someone who has directly communicated with God and is authorized to speak for him. A high priest is God's appointed person to represent the people to Himself. Jesus is both God's spokesman and our representative to God.

Christ is without sin and evil. Because of this, He became the only perfect man to walk upon the earth. Therefore, He is the only one who could die to save us.

Jesus is our only source of hope in the world. His conquest of death gives us confidence now and for the future.

Because Christ and the Father are one in nature, Jesus perfectly reflects God. When we look at Him, we see what God looks like as a man.

Jesus is the Greek form of the Hebrew *Yeshua* (Joshua). The name means "Yahweh (Jehovah) is salvation."

Jesus, the very one who is our Advocate before the bar of God's justice, has been made the Judge of all. (Romans 8:33, 34)

Related Titles (by root word and/or theme)

Head of the Creation of God (Revelation 3:14)

Amen (Revelation 3:14)
Faithful and True (Revelation 19:11)
Truth (John 14:6)

Firstfruits (1 Corinthians 15:20)
Firstborn from the Dead (Colossians 1:18)

Fullness of God (Colossians 2:9)
See *Son of God* and *Yahweh*.

Head of the Body (Ephesians 4:15, 16)
See *Bridegroom*.

Bishop of Souls, Minister of the Sanctuary, the Prophet (1 Peter 2:25; Hebrews 8:1-2; Deuteronomy 18:15, 18; John 6:14)

Holy Child, Lord Our Righteousness, Righteous One, Sanctification (Acts 4:30, Jeremiah 23:5, 6; 1 John 2:1; 1 Corinthians 1:30)

Hope of Glory (Colossians 1:27)
Hope of Israel (Jeremiah 17:13)

Exact Representation of His Nature (Hebrews 1:3)

Yeshua (Joshua)

See *Wonderful Counselor*.

Name	References	Meaning
KING OF KINGS	Revelation 17:14	Jesus is king over all.
LAMB OF GOD	John 1:29, 36; 1 Peter 1:19; Rev. 5:6-12; 7:17	Jesus is our sacrifice.
LAST ADAM	1 Corinthians 15:45	Jesus is the Father of a new human nature.
LIGHT OF THE WORLD	John 8:12	Jesus is the light.
LION OF THE TRIBE OF JUDAH	Genesis 49:9, 10; Revelation 5:5	Jesus is David's son.
LIVING WATER SPIRIT	John 4:10; 7:38	Jesus is our spiritual drink.
LORD OF LORDS	Revelation 19:16; 1 Timothy 6:15	Jesus is Lord.
MAN OF SORROWS	Isaiah 53:3	Jesus bore our sorrows.
MASTER	Matthew 8:19	Jesus is our teacher.
MESSENGER OF THE COVENANT	Malachi 3:1	Jesus is God's final messenger.
MESSIAH	Daniel 9:25; John 1:41; 4:25	Jesus is Messiah.

Insights	Related Titles (by root word and/or theme)
Christ is the king over all kings and rulers. As subjects in His kingdom, we owe Him our complete allegiance.	King, King of Israel, King of the Jews, Lord of Lords, Master, Prince, Ruler Sovereign (Matt. 21:5; Jn. 1:49; Matt. 2:2; Rev. 19:16; Lk. 8:24; Dan. 9:25; 1 Tim. 6:15)
Jesus is the fulfillment of the whole sacrificial system (Hebrews 7:26-29), especially as our Passover Lamb. As the Lamb of God, Jesus' sacrifice pays for our sins past, present, and future.	Offering (Hebrews 10:10) Passover (1 Corinthians 5:7) Propitiation (1 John 2:2) Sacrifice (Ephesians 5:2)
The first Adam brought sin and death. Jesus is the Last Adam, bringing life. From Him flows eternal life.	Man, Second Man, Son of Man (John 19:5; 1 Timothy 2:5; Daniel 7:13-14; Mark 9:31)
Jesus' radiance reveals God. Knowing Jesus is to know and see what God is like. Those who follow Him will not walk in darkness (John 8:12).	Light, Radiance of God's Glory (John 1:4, 5; Hebrews 1:3) See *Bright Morning Star.*
Jesus fulfills the Old Testament prophecies, being from the tribe of Judah and the lineage of David.	Son of David (Matthew 12:23) See *King of Kings.*
Christ is the fountainhead of the life that wells up inside every believer like an unending spring.	Fountain Life-Giving Spirit (Jeremiah 2:13; Zechariah 13:1; 1 Cor. 15:45)
Jesus is Lord over all! He has this title by right as the Son of God and Creator of the cosmos. It is also a title He has earned by His humble work of becoming human in order to redeem us through His death.	Lord (Philippians 2:11) See *King of Kings.*
Jesus did not come to enjoy a life of happy kingship over the world. He came to carry the world's sins and sorrows, that we might have eternal joy with Him and God the Father.	Servant, Slave (Isaiah 42:1, 2; 49:7; 52:13–53:12; Matthew 12:18-20)
Master means "teacher" or "rabbi." Jesus is the final source of truth concerning God. He is the only teacher who can show us the way to go.	Rabbi, Rabboni, Teacher, Truth (John 20:16; John 14:6, 7)
Messenger and *angel* are the same word in both the Old and New Testaments. Christ is God's ultimate messenger of the New Covenant of God's grace and head of God's angelic armies.	Angel of the Lord, Captain of the Lord's Host (Exodus 3:2; Judges 13:15-18; Joshua 5:14)
Messiah is the Hebrew word, translated into Greek, as *Christ.* Both words mean "Anointed One" (one especially appointed by God for His plan and purpose).	Christ, Anointed One (Matthew 1:16; Psalm 2:1, 2)

Name	References	Meaning
PRINCE OF PEACE	Isaiah 9:6	Jesus is our peace.
PROPHET	John 6:14; 7:40; Deuteronomy 18:15-22; Luke 7:16; Matthew 21:11	Jesus is the prophet foretold.
REDEEMER	Job 19:25	Jesus is our redemption.
RESURRECTION AND THE LIFE	John 11:25	Jesus is life.
SAVIOR	Luke 1:47-2:11; John 4:42; 1 John 4:14	Jesus is our salvation.
SHEPHERD	1 Peter 2:25	Jesus is the good shepherd.
SHILOH	Genesis 49:10	Jesus is our promised peace.
SON OF GOD	Luke 1:35; Hebrews 4:14	Jesus is the Son of God by nature.
TRUE VINE	John 15:1	Jesus is our evergreen source of life.
THE WAY, THE TRUTH, AND THE LIFE	John 14:6; Acts 9:2	Jesus is our path to God.

Insights

Related Titles (by root word and/or theme)

Christ is our peace. He has ended the conflict between God and man by His death on the cross. He has also given us internal peace by the love that is planted in our hearts by His Spirit.

Peace (Ephesians 2:14)
King of Salem (Hebrews 7:1, 2)

Long before Jesus was born, Moses and others prophesied that a prophet like him would come speaking God's words. Jesus is that Prophet, the ultimate and final spokesman for God.

See *High Priest.*

Christ's death is the payment that redeems us from the debt we owe to God's law, ransoming our lives and guaranteeing us a place in His family.

Kinsman, Ransom, Redemption, Guarantee (Ruth 2:14; Matthew 20:28; 1 Timothy 2:6; 1 Corinthians 1:30; Hebrews 7:22)

Christ is Life itself. Death could not hold Him, nor can it hold any who are in Him.

Living One (Revelation 1:18)
See *Firstborn.*

Christ is the Savior of the world who came to deliver us from the power of death. He is the one who seeks and saves the lost.

Captain of Salvation, Deliverer, Horn of Salvation, Salvation (Hebrews 2:10; Romans 11:26; Luke 1:69; 2:30)

Jesus came to care for and to lead lost sheep, lost men and women. His sheep know His voice and no one can take them from His hands.

Door of the Sheepfold, Good Shepherd (John 10:7, 14) See *Door.*

Shiloh may be translated as "to whom the scepter belongs," or as a name derived from the Hebrew word for peace. Jesus fulfills the prophecy by being the King to whom the scepter belongs and our Prince of Peace.

See *Messiah* and *Prince of Peace.*

Christ is the only "natural" Son of God, which means He partakes in the Divine nature fully. We become God's children by adoption and inherit all creation in, and with, Christ.

Only Begotten, Son of the Most High, Heir (John 1:14, 18; Luke 1:32; Hebrews 1:2) See *God.*

Jesus is our connection to the source of life. As God He has life in Himself. Having become a man He extends that life to all who believe.

See *Branch.*

Jesus is the Way to God. He is the path to truth and life. No mere human teacher, He is the map, the road, the destination and the one who has gone ahead of us.

Forerunner, Jacob's Ladder (Hebrews 6:20; Genesis 28:12; John 1:51)

Name	References	Meaning
WISDOM OF GOD	1 Corinthians 1:24, 30	Jesus is our wisdom from God.
WONDERFUL COUNSELOR	Isaiah 9:6	Jesus is our defense attorney.
WORD	John 1:1, 14	Jesus is God's Word.
YAHWEH (JEHOVAH*)	Isaiah 40:3-5; Matthew 3:3; 28:19; Philippians 2:6-11; Exodus 3:14	Jesus has God's name.

Names of God	Meaning	References
YAHWEH*-YIREH	God Will Provide	Genesis 22:13, 14
YAHWEH-MEKADDISHKEM	The Lord Who Sanctifies	Exodus 31:12, 13
YAHWEH-NISSI	The Lord is My Banner	Exodus 17:15, 16
YAHWEH-RAPHA	The Lord Who Heals	Exodus 15:25-27
YAHWEH-ROHI	The Lord is My Shepherd	Psalm 23:1-3
YAHWEH-SABAOTH	The Lord of Hosts	1 Samuel 1:3
YAHWEH-SHALOM	The Lord is Peace	Numbers 6:22-27
YAHWEH-SHAMMAH	The Lord is There	Ezekiel 48:35
YAHWEH-TSIDKANU	The Lord Our Righteousness	Jeremiah 23:5, 6; 33:16

*Using the vowels of Adonai (Lord) and the consonants of YHVH (God), a 16th-century German translator incorrectly translated YHVH as YaHoVah, resulting in the name Jehovah. Yahweh is the more accepted spelling for God's name.

Insights

Though the reference in Proverbs is not a strict prophetic word about Christ, the concept of wisdom as a person and associate of God is fulfilled in Jesus. To know Jesus is to be connected to the wisdom of the ages.

Christ is our Wonderful Counselor before God. He comforts, consoles and counsels us as our Mediator and Intercessor. As our Advocate before God, He defends us like a lawyer before the bar of God's justice, offering Himself as a payment for our crimes.

Jesus is the speech uttered by God the Father, impelled by the breath of God's Spirit. He is not merely information, but the effective, powerful Word that calls creation out of nothing and life out of death.

The holy name *Yahweh* means "He who is." It expresses the idea that only God has self-existent being. The name was so holy that the Jews would not utter it out loud. Christ possesses this name.

Related Titles (by root word and/or theme)

Compare personified wisdom
(Proverbs 8:22-31; Luke 11:49)

Advocate, Comforter, Consolation of Israel, Daysman, Intercessor, Mediator, Paraclete (1 John 2:1; John 14:16; Luke 2:25; Job 9:33; 1 Timothy 2:5) See *Judge*.

Word of God, Word of Life
(1 John 1:1)

I AM; Who was, Who is and Who is to come (Mark 6:50; Luke 21:8; John 8:24, 28, 58; Revelation 4:8)

Parallel Verses Referring to Jesus

"I am the bread of life." (John 6:35)

We have been made holy by the blood of Jesus. (Hebrews 13:12)

Jesus, the root of Jesse, is our banner. (Isaiah 11:10)

By His stripes we are healed. (1 Peter 2:24)

"I am the good Shepherd." (John 10:11)

Jesus will come as King of Kings. (Revelation 1:8)

Jesus is the Prince of Peace. (Isaiah 9:6)

Jesus said that He will be present in our hearts. (Matthew 28:20)

Because of Jesus, we are righteous before God. (2 Corinthians 5:21)

WHAT DOES IT MEAN TO PRAY IN JESUS' NAME?

Jesus himself instructed us to do it (John 16:24), but do we understand it? To pray in Jesus' name means to pray in the authority of that name, much as we might use the phrase "in the name of the law" to assert the authority of the law. But the use of Jesus' name should be more than a mere postscript on our prayers, more even than an authoritative letterhead. To pray effectively in Christ's name, we must be "in Him"—in union with his life and death. In his letters, Paul uses the prepositions "in" and "together with" to emphasize the connectedness of the believer to Christ and His authority and power.

Praying in Jesus' name does not give our prayers extra power. The truth is, prayers are completely powerless in the first place unless they are "in Jesus." Without Christ's intercession, no prayers would make it to the ears of God. The reason we are told to pray in and by his authority is not as some magic formula, but to put our own spirits and our own thinking in the right place—under and in him.

"No" for an Answer

Of course this means we must be willing to accept "no" as an answer. Even God's "no" is not a "No way," but "No, I have something better in mind." Christ's prayer in Gethsemane before His crucifixion should teach us both about whose authority we are under and about accepting God's better plan (Matthew 26:39; Mark 14:36; Luke 22:42). Christ invites us to pray in his name, assuring us that whatever is asked, by his authority and in faith, will be granted by God. This means that, first, we must be connected to God in Christ, and second, that we must know we have what we ask.

For Christians, the second part is often difficult, even impossible. Christ's Gethsemane prayer ("Let this cup pass from me"), the only request He made that was denied, teaches us that there are some things we ask for—good as they may seem—that are not God's best for us. Jesus knew it was the Father's will that He should suffer on our behalf; many of our prayers may also fall into this category. But observe the powerful results: In Jesus' case, as in ours, the ultimate outcome will be life out of death.

We should think of our prayers as Christ's own prayers through us, inspired and led by the Holy Spirit. God has already planned out the good works we are to walk in; these include our prayers (Ephesians 2:10). Seeing our prayers as Jesus' prayers *through us* should cause us to rethink what we ask for. It should also cause us to think about our union with Christ. Real authority always flows from the author. Are we connected to the Author and Perfecter of our faith?

Author: William Brent Ashby, BT

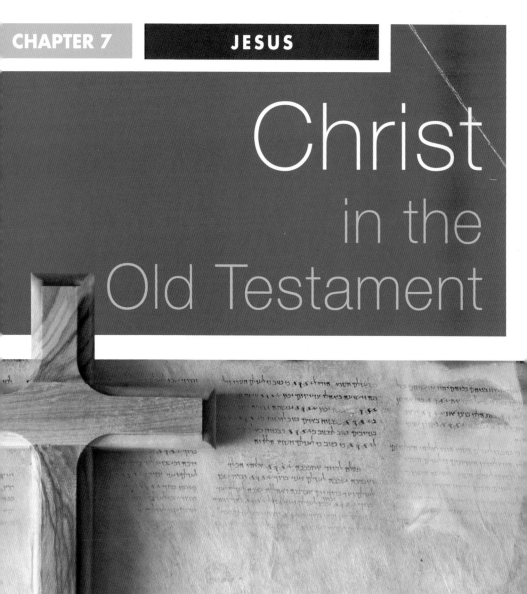

Christ
in the
Old Testament

13 Old Testament People Who
Foreshadowed Christ

20 Prophecies Fulfilled by Jesus

CHRIST IN THE OLD TESTAMENT

THE NEW TESTAMENT IS IN THE OLD CONCEALED; THE OLD TESTAMENT IS IN THE NEW REVEALED.

—Augustine

CHRIST is the key to what God had been pointing to in all the history of God's people.

One way to see this is to examine parallels between Old Testament people, events, and things, and the life of Jesus in the New Testament.

We find some of these parallels in Romans 5. Paul writes that sin entered into the world through one man, Adam, and sin led to death for all men, for all have sinned. He also writes that Adam was a figure of someone who was to come (Romans 5:12).

Paul said that if the sin of one person, Adam, would cause many to die, how much more could the gift of God's grace, by one person—Jesus Christ, cause many to be righteous and have eternal life!

The Bible is full of these parallels or "types." The study of "types" is called typology. In the example above, this method (typology) calls Adam the type and Christ the antitype (opposite). Typology was a very common way to interpret the Old Testament in the early history of the church. When carefully done, typology opens windows into the history of God's activity in the world that otherwise can be easily missed.

By looking for parallels or similarities between biblical people, events (for example, the Exodus anticipates how Christ frees us from the slavery of sin), and things (for example, the tabernacle, which John 1:14 connects with Jesus), we can see God setting up history for the coming of Christ and doing it not simply by speaking a prophetic word, but by arranging the affairs of human beings. When we understand this great truth, we can hope to believe our own lives too point to Christ, and joy in the Lord of history who makes such wonderful stories of us!

Adam

ADAM (Genesis 2–3)

Adam was the first human God created. He was responsible to care for the Garden of Eden. His disobedience of God's commandment introduced sin and death, so humanity and all of creation became corrupted by sin.

ADAM	CHRIST
Adam was the first person in this creation.	In his resurrection, Jesus is the first person in this New Creation (1 Corinthians 15:23).
Adam was called the son of God (Luke 3:38).	Christ is the Son of God (John 1:14).
Adam was God's administrator or ruler (Genesis 1:28).	Christ is God's Anointed to be King (Matthew 1:16).
Adam was the head of the race (Genesis 3:20).	Christ Jesus is the Head of the New Creation (Romans 5:12–24).
His actions brought consequences to his children causing them to inherit sin and death (Genesis 3:16–19).	His actions brought consequences to God's children causing them to inherit righteousness and life (Romans 5:12–19, 1 Corinthians 15:20–22, 45–49).
Adam joined Eve and rebelled against God (Genesis 3:6).	Christ redeemed his bride (the church) by obeying God (Revelation 19:7–9).
Adam's shame required the death of an animal to cover it (Genesis 3:21).	Christ was shamed, stripped and slain to cover our shame (Matthew 27:27–35).
Instead of closeness with God, we experience isolation and loneliness. Instead of love and care for each other, we experience violence and hatred.	Through Christ's redemptive action, we can experience true life, a close relationship with God and his love, and care for others.

QUESTIONS

Because of Adam's sin, the good world God made became corrupt. How does Christ "fix" what Adam "broke?" (Romans 5:15–19)

ADAM is a good first example of a *type*. It shows very clearly that typology focuses on specific events or character traits rather than on the person as a whole. There are big differences between Adam and Christ; in fact, they are opposites of one another. So it is not that Adam was *like* Christ; rather, some features of his story *parallel* Christ's life and ministry. Some are positive and others are negative.

Noah

NOAH (Genesis 6–9)

When God had decided to destroy the world with a flood as a punishment for humanity's sin, God chose Noah and his family to save them from the flood. Noah built an ark to save the animals.

NOAH	CHRIST
Noah was a kind of "second Adam" since all living human beings come from him (Genesis 8:15–9:17).	Christ is called "the second man" (Adam) since eternal life can only be found in him (1 Corinthians 15:47).
Noah's ark provided refuge for all kinds of animals (Genesis 6:19–7:5).	Christ's body (the church) provides salvation for all, both Jew and Gentile (Romans 11:11; Galatians 3:28–29).
Human evil had reached an unacceptable high. So God decided to undo his creation with a flood (Genesis 6:6–7).	When the time is right for God, he will undo his creation by fire (2 Peter 3:12–13) to re-create it (Revelation 21:1).
Noah's ark was delivered from the flood waters (Genesis 7:7).	Christ's body (the church) was delivered from death through the water of baptism (1 Peter 3:21).
Noah offered a sacrifice of blood (Genesis 8:20–9:6).	Christ offered himself as a sacrifice (1 Peter 1:18–19).
Noah's ark came to rest on Mount Ararat on the Jewish month of Nisan 17 (Genesis 8:4).	Christ's resurrection took place on Nisan 17 (which corresponds to the month of March or April).
Although Noah was not perfect, he is described as a "righteous man, blameless among the people of his time, and he walked with God" (Genesis 6:9).	Jesus was the perfect, blameless man (Hebrews 4:15).

QUESTIONS

Each of us is a bit like Noah. See 2 Peter 3:12–14. We too know this world will end. How should we live today?

What made Noah a "righteous man" even though his life was far from perfect?

Abraham

ABRAHAM (Genesis 12–25)

God chose Abraham and commanded him to leave his home and travel to an unknown place. God promised Abraham that he would be the father of a great nation and that Sarah, his wife, would give him a son. Through this son, God would bless all the nations. When they were elderly, Abraham and Sarah had Isaac, the son of the promise.

ABRAHAM	CHRIST
Abraham is called the "Father of the Faith" (Genesis 15; Romans 4:16–18).	Christ is the author and perfecter of faith (Hebrews 12:2).
Abraham was willing to sacrifice his only son (Genesis 22:2), and Isaac was ready to do what his father said (Genesis 22:9).	God the Father was willing to sacrifice his only Son (John 3:16) and Jesus was ready to do what his Father said (John 10:17–18).
Abraham's faith allowed him to trust that God would keep his word, even if that meant raising Isaac from the dead.	As Abraham's faith allowed him to look forward to Jesus' own resurrection with hope, we now look backwards to that same resurrection that gives us hope (1 Corinthians 15:54–58).
Abraham's sacrifice took place on Mount Moriah (Jerusalem; Genesis 22:2, 2 Chronicles 3:1) and a ram was substituted for Isaac (Genesis 22:8, 13–14).	Christ was sacrificed on the outskirts of Jerusalem (John 19:17–18) and he is the Lamb of God (John 1:29–31).
Abraham's son (Isaac) was the child of the promise. The book of Hebrews connected Isaac to the idea of resurrection (Hebrews 11:17–19).	God's Son Jesus is the child of promise (Isaiah 9:6) who is resurrected (1 Corinthians 15:1–11).
In Isaac's birth, all nations were to be blessed (Genesis 12:3).	In Jesus Christ all nations are blessed (Acts 28:28, Matthew 28:18–20).

QUESTIONS

Throughout the Bible, there is a theme of sacrificing lives, wishes, and desires. How could Abraham's story help you in your faith journey?

Melchizedek

MELCHIZEDEK (Genesis 14:18-20)

After Abraham came back from fighting enemy armies to free Lot, his nephew, Melchizedek, king of Salem, met him on the road with a gift of bread and wine. Abraham recognized him as a fellow believer and priest of the true God by giving to him one tenth of his earnings, which was the king's share (see 1 Samuel 8:15, 17).

MELCHIZEDEK	CHRIST
Melchizedek's name means "king of righteousness."	Christ is the Righteous One (Acts 3:14; Jeremiah 23:5-6).
Melchizedek was king of Salem (Jerusalem). The word "salem" means peace (Genesis 14:18; Hebrews 7:2). He was king before David.	He is the Prince of Peace (Isaiah 9:6) and the rightful king of Jerusalem for all time.
Melchizedek was a priest of God Most High (Genesis 14:18) before Aaron and the Levitical priesthood. (Aaron and his sons were ordained as the priestly family for Israel in Leviticus 8.)	Christ's High priesthood precedes and is superior to any other priesthood—that is, the priesthood of Aaron in Leviticus 8 and of Melchizedek in Genesis 14 (see Hebrews 7:4-10).
Old Testament priests offered blessings for God's people (see Numbers 6:22-27).	As High Priest (Hebrews 7:4-10), Christ blesses God's people with every spiritual blessing (Ephesians 1:3).
Melchizedek blesses Abraham on God's behalf (Genesis 14:19-20).	Christ blesses us, Abraham's spiritual children (Galatians 3:29).

QUESTIONS

Read Hebrews 8. What does it mean that Christ is high priest?

Ephesians 1:3 says that believers are blessed with every spiritual blessing. List some "spiritual blessings" that you have seen in your life in the past week.

Joseph

JOSEPH (Genesis 37–50)

Joseph was a son of Jacob and Rachel (Genesis 35:24). After Joseph's jealous brothers threw him into a pit, he was taken to Egypt and sold as a slave. In Egypt, God blessed Joseph, who became second only to the king of Egypt. God used Joseph to bless the nations by wisely storing grain in times of abundance so they were ready for the famine to come.

JOSEPH	CHRIST
Joseph was rejected by his own brothers (Genesis 37:19-20), stripped of his robe, and thrown into a pit (Genesis 37:22-24). Sold into slavery, he eventually landed in a dungeon in Egypt (Genesis 37:28 and 39:20).	Christ was rejected by his own (John 1:11). He was stripped of his robe, condemned to death and descended to hell (Matthew 27:27-31; John 19:23-24; 1 Peter 3:18-20).
Joseph was an exemplary servant (Genesis 39:1-6). Though he was tempted he did not give in to temptation (Genesis 39:7-12).	Christ came as a servant (Philippians 2:7). He was tempted, but did not sin (Hebrews 4:15).
Joseph was unjustly accused and condemned (Genesis 39:13-20). In prison Joseph interpreted a dream of life to one of his fellow prisoners and death to another (Genesis 40:6-23). He was raised out of the dungeon to sit at Pharaoh's right hand (Genesis 41:14-45).	Christ was unjustly accused and condemned (Matthew 26:57-68; 27:11-25). While on the cross, Jesus' words promise life to one of the thieves condemned with him (Luke 23:39-43). Jesus was raised from the prison of death to sit at the right hand of God the Father (Acts 2:33; 5:31).
Joseph had a meal with his brothers before he revealed himself to them (Genesis 43:16). When he did reveal himself, Joseph saved his brothers' lives (Genesis 45:3-15). Joseph's actions also saved Egypt and many others (Genesis 50:20).	Jesus had a last supper with his disciples (Matthew 26:17-30). After his death and resurrection he revealed himself to them alive, which brought about salvation for them and the world (Luke 24; 1 Corinthians 15:1-11).
In Joseph, God partially fulfilled his promise to Abraham to bless all the nations of the world (Genesis 12:1-3), since Joseph's actions helped the nations of the world survive the terrible famine (Genesis 41:57).	In Christ, God completely fulfilled his promise to Abraham (Genesis 12:1-3), since Christ died for the sins of the world, and Jesus commanded: "go and make disciples of all nations...." (Matthew 28:19).

QUESTIONS

Joseph was abused, betrayed, and mistreated, yet he (like Christ) was a blessing even to those who hurt him. How does this apply to your life?

Moses

MOSES (Exodus–Deuteronomy)

God called Moses to lead the Israelites out of Egypt. Moses became Israel's leader, prophet, and judge. He went with Israel from Egypt to the Promised Land in Canaan and during the wanderings in the desert. God gave his Law to Israel through Moses.

MOSES	CHRIST
Surrounding the birth of Moses, innocent children were killed by Pharaoh (Exodus 1:22).	Surrounding the birth of Jesus, King Herod killed innocent children in Bethlehem (Matthew 2:16).
Moses had to flee his natural land because of Pharaoh's persecution (Exodus 2:15).	Jesus and his family had to flee their native land because of Herod's persecution (Matthew 2:14).
Pharaoh died and Moses returned after he is told: "All the men are dead that sought your life" (Exodus 4:19).	Herod died and Jesus returned after "...those who sought the child's life are dead" (Matthew 2:20-21).
Moses' prayer healed Miriam of leprosy (Numbers 12:10-13).	Jesus cleansed the leper (Matthew 8:2-3).
Moses chose 12 messengers, one from each tribe. Hoshea, who becomes Moses' close associate, is renamed Joshua (Numbers 13:2-16).	Jesus chose 12 apostles who will judge Israel's 12 tribes. Simon, one of those closest to Jesus, was renamed Peter (Matthew 16:17-19; Mark 3:16-17).
Moses prayed over the miracle of the manna and quails (Exodus 16:1; Numbers 11:31).	Jesus performed the miracle of the loaves and fish twice (Matthew 14:13-21; 15:32-39).
The dividing of the Red Sea took place under Moses' command (Exodus 14:15-22).	Jesus walked on the sea and calmed the storm (Matthew 14:22-36).
Moses was on a mountain for the blessing of the commandments (Exodus 19:20; Deuteronomy 6:5-25).	Jesus was on a mount when he gave the Beatitudes and his commandments (Matthew 5:1-12).
A cloud overshadowed Moses, Aaron and Miriam and the voice of God was heard (Numbers 12:5-8).	A cloud overshadowed Peter, James, and John with Jesus, and the voice of God was heard (Matthew 17:1-5).
God promised to raise up a prophet like Moses (Deuteronomy 18:15).	Christ is the prophet that God promised, but he is greater than Moses (Hebrews 3:1-6).
Although Moses brought Israel to the border of the Promised Land, as a punishment for his own rebellion, he could not enter it (Num. 20:1-13).	Because of his obedience, Jesus brings people into Paradise (Luke 23:43).

QUESTIONS

Examine the story of Moses and the rock (Numbers 20:1–13).
Why did God punish Moses so harshly?

Even Moses, the giver of the Law, was not able to perfectly obey the Law. Jesus perfectly obeyed the Law. What does Jesus' perfect obedience mean for us today? (Phil. 2:8).

Joshua

JOSHUA (Numbers 27:12–23; Deuteronomy 31:1–8; Book of Joshua)

Joshua, whose earlier name was Hoshea, was one of the twelve spies that Moses sent to "explore the land of Canaan." Only he and Caleb encouraged the people to trust God and take possession of the land of Canaan, which God had promised to Abraham. When Moses died, Joshua became the leader who brought Israel into the land of Canaan.

JOSHUA	CHRIST
Joshua's name is actually the same name as Jesus: "Yehoshua," or "Yeshua" for short, means "The LORD saves."	Jesus' name is the Greek form of the name Yeshua. Like Joshua, Jesus led his people into salvation, yet in a greater sense of eternal life.
Joshua was God's prophetic leader who stepped into Moses' shoes (Joshua 1:1–9).	Jesus fulfilled Moses' prophecy: "The Lord your God will raise up for you a prophet like me from among you...." (Deuteronomy 18:15; see also, Acts 3:22–23).
Joshua parted the Jordan river so that Israel could cross over (Joshua 3:7–17).	Jesus walked on water and called others to come over to him (Matthew 14:25–29).
Joshua led God's people into the Promised Land, the inheritance God promised to Abraham (Joshua 1:2–3).	Jesus leads God's people into the Promised Land, his inheritance (Matthew 25:34, Ephesians 1:13–14).
Joshua's army pulled down earthly strongholds (Joshua 6).	Jesus' army pulls down spiritual strongholds (2 Corinthians 10:3–5).
Joshua's army was arrayed in earthly armor (Joshua 6:9).	Jesus' army is arrayed in spiritual armor (Ephesians 6:10–17).
Joshua described himself as God's servant (Joshua 24:15).	Jesus described himself as a servant (Luke 22:27; John 13:1–17; Philippians 2:7).
Joshua led God's people to rest in the Promised Land (Joshua 21:44).	Jesus' followers are led into rest in this new creation (Hebrews 4:1).

QUESTIONS

Joshua's army was armed for physical battle, but Jesus' followers are armed for spiritual battle. Discuss the spiritual armor that God has given us in Ephesians 6:10–17.

Samuel

SAMUEL (1 and 2 Samuel)

Samuel was a prophet of God at the end of the days of the Judges. Samuel guided the people of Israel when there was still no king. When God allowed the existence of a king in Israel, Samuel anointed Saul to be king. When God rejected Saul and chose David as the new king, Samuel also anointed David.

SAMUEL	CHRIST
Samuel's mother Hannah was blessed by the High Priest Eli before the birth of Samuel (1 Samuel 1:17).	Mary, the mother of Jesus, was blessed by an angel before the birth of Jesus (Luke 1:30).
Samuel's mother, Hannah, uttered a prayer praising God for goodness to her. This took place in the presence of the priest Eli (1 Samuel 2:1–11).	Jesus' mother Mary spoke a lengthy prayer in the priestly house of Zechariah and Elizabeth. This prayer is remarkably similar to Hannah's prayer (Luke 1:46-56).
After nursing Samuel, Hannah brought him to the tabernacle with a sacrifice to dedicate him to God (1 Samuel 1:24–28). Eli received the child (1 Samuel 1:23).	After a period of purification, Mary and Joseph brought Jesus to the temple with an offering (Luke 2:22–24). Simeon received the child (Luke 2:25–28).
The parents went up every year to the tabernacle (1 Samuel 2:19).	The parents went up every year to the temple (Luke 2:41).
The child, Samuel, sat and served in the tabernacle (1 Samuel 2:18; 3:21).	The child, Jesus, sat and served in the temple (Luke 2:46–50).
"And the child, Samuel, grew and increased in favor, both with the Lord, and also with men" (1 Samuel 2:26).	"And Jesus grew in wisdom and stature, and in favor with God and man" (Luke 2:52).
Samuel was given to Israel after a long silence from God (1 Samuel 3:1).	Jesus was given to Israel after a long silence from God.
Samuel partially fulfilled God's promise of raising a prophet like Moses (Deuteronomy 18:15; 1 Samuel 3:19-21).	Christ is the ultimate fulfillment of God's promise to raise a prophet like Moses. However, Jesus is greater than Moses (Hebrews 3:1–6).
Samuel established the position of kingship in Israel (1 Samuel 10:24–25).	Jesus established the true kingship of Israel and the world (Luke 1:32–33).

QUESTIONS

Being in favor with God means to please God. Read 1 Thessalonians 4:1–12 and discuss different ways to please God.

DAVID (1 and 2 Samuel)

David was a shepherd who bravely faced and killed Goliath, a Philistine enemy of Israel. Eventually, God chose David to become king of Israel after Saul. King David settled Israel in the conquered land of Canaan and expanded the kingdom. Despite David's sins, God called David "a man after my own heart" (1 Samuel 13:14 and Acts 13:22).

DAVID	CHRIST
God gave David victory against Goliath (1 Samuel 17:45–47).	God gave Christ victory over death (1 Corinthians 6:14).
David was pursued by Saul, the rejected king of Israel (1 Samuel 19).	Jesus was pursued by Herod, the illegitimate king of Judah (Matthew 2:13–18).
David's enemies came after him, but were overpowered by the Holy Spirit (1 Samuel 19:18–24).	Jesus' enemies came to arrest him and were overpowered by the Holy Spirit at Jesus' word (John 18:1–11).
David had a friend and advocate in Jonathan who spoke up for David at the risk of his own life (1 Samuel 20).	Jesus had a friend and advocate in John the Baptist who spoke up for Jesus at the risk of his own life (John 3:22–30).
David's hungry men ate the bread of the Presence (1 Samuel 21:1–6).	Jesus' hungry disciples ate grain on the Sabbath (Matthew 12:1–8).
David was tempted and fell (2 Samuel 11).	Jesus was tempted and did not fall (Hebrews 4:15).
Even with David's imperfections, God loved David and made a covenant with him (2 Samuel 7:11–16).	Christ, in his love for humanity, made a new covenant (Matthew 26:28; Hebrews 12:24).
David's son, Solomon, whose name means "Peace," inherited David's throne (1 King 1:29–30).	David's offspring, Jesus, is called the Prince of Peace and he holds David's throne forever (Isaiah 9:6; Luke 1:31–33).
David's experiences are reflected in the Psalms: Psalm 22, Psalm 31, Psalm 32, Psalm 35, Psalm 40, Psalm 41, Psalm 45, Psalm 68, Psalm 69, Psalm 109, Psalm 110.	Jesus' experiences are fulfillments of these Psalms: Psalm 22, Psalm 31, Psalm 32, Psalm 35, Psalm 40, Psalm 41, Psalm 45, Psalm 68, Psalm 69, Psalm 109, Psalm 110.

QUESTIONS

In Psalm 22 David expressed the feeling that God abandoned him and lamented for it. Jesus repeated it while he was hanging on the cross. Have you ever felt as if God has abandoned you?
In the previous Psalms, which feelings or experiences can you identify with?

Elijah, Elisha

ELIJAH AND ELISHA (1 Kings 17—2 Kings 9)

Elijah was a prophet who confronted the king and queen with their sin. He also called all of Israel to repent and obey the Lord. God showed his power through Elijah's ministry. Elijah chose Elisha as his successor as a prophet in Israel. As with Elijah, God demonstrated his power through Elisha's ministry.

ELIJAH & ELISHA	CHRIST
Elijah's call to repentance on behalf of God came at a time of great unfaithfulness (1 Kings 19:14-18).	Christ's announcement of the kingdom of God came at precisely the time God had prepared (Mark 1:15).
While in the desert, ravens took care of Elijah (1 Kings 17:6). At another time in the wilderness traveling on a 40-day journey, an angel fed him (1 Kings 19:3-8).	Jesus was tempted in the desert after a 40-day fast. Angels took care of him (Matthew 4:2, 11; Mark 1:13; Luke 4:2).
Elijah called his disciple Elisha, who left his oxen and home to follow Elijah (1 Kings 19:19-21).	Jesus called his disciples and they immediately left their homes and fishing (Matthew 4:18-22).
Elijah raised a widow's son from the dead and gave him back to his mother (1 Kings 17:17-24).	Jesus raised a widow's son in the town of Nain and gave him back to his mother (Luke 7:11-17).
Elijah called down fire from heaven on his enemies (2 Kings 1:12).	Jesus refused to let his disciples call fire from heaven on his enemies (Luke 9:52-56).
Elisha cleansed the leper Naaman (2 Kings 5:1-19).	Jesus cleansed the leper (Matthew 8:1-3; Mark 1:40-42; Luke 5:12-13).
Elisha raised a prominent woman's son from the dead (2 Kings 4:8-37).	Jesus raised a prominent man's daughter from the dead (Matt. 9:23-25; Mk. 5:35-42; Lk. 8:41-55).
Elisha multiplied food on two separate occasions (2 Kings 4:1-7; 42-44).	Jesus multiplied food on two separate occasions (Matthew 14:13-21; 15:29-39).
A person was resurrected when he was thrown into Elisha's tomb and touched his bones (2 Kings 13:21).	A woman was healed when she touched Jesus' garments (Matthew 9:18-22).

QUESTIONS

At one point when Elijah felt alone and defeated, God showed him that God had preserved his faithful people. God let Elijah know he was not alone. When have you felt alone, misunderstood, ready to give up, like Elijah did? How does Elijah's story in 1 Kings 19:3–18 help you deal with these moments?

Elisha's response to Elijah's calling was to drop everything and follow him. Jesus' disciples had a similar response to his call. What does it mean for the church today? How is God calling us to serve him?

Zerubbabel, Joshua

ZERUBBABEL AND JOSHUA (Ezra 3–6; Zechariah 3–6)

As a punishment for Israel's rebellion, God allowed the Babylonian Empire to destroy Jerusalem, the temple, and take the Jews captive to Babylon. After 70 years, God allowed the Jews to return to Jerusalem. One of the tasks the Jews had was to rebuild the temple. Zerubbabel (a descendant of David) and Joshua (a high priest) were the leaders that God chose to accomplish this task.

ZERUBBABEL & JOSHUA	CHRIST
Zerubbabel was the son of David, heir to the throne and leader of Israel in his day (Ezra 2:1–2; see Matthew 1:13 and Luke 3:27).	Jesus is the son of David and King of Israel. He is the leader of all God's people (Luke 1:32–33).
Zerubbabel helped lay the foundation and completed the second temple (Zechariah 4:9; Ezra 3:11, 6:14–15).	Jesus' body, which was raised from the ground, is the new temple and his people are called a "body," which is that "temple" on earth (John 2:19–22; Romans 12:5; 1 Corinthians 12:27; 1 Corinthians 3:10; Ephesians 2:21).
Zerubbabel laid the capstone of the rebuilt temple to shouts of "Grace, grace to it" (Zechariah 4:7).	Jesus is called the cornerstone (Acts 4:11; Ephesians 2:20; 1 Peter 2:7). He is the foundation and source of God's grace (John 1:17).
Joshua was the high priest in Israel at the time the temple was about to be rebuilt (Zechariah 3:1).	Jesus' name is the New Testament Greek form of the Old Testament Hebrew name Joshua. He is the true and ultimate High Priest (Hebrews 7).
God clothed Joshua with clean garments so he could stand in the presence of the Holy God (Zechariah 3:3–5).	Christ clothes us with his righteousness (Galatians 3:27). He is standing in the heavenly temple in the robes of the Great High Priest (Revelations 1:12–18).
Satan tried to accuse him, but God himself defended Joshua (Zechariah 3:1–5).	Satan tried to destroy Jesus, but Jesus defeated Satan (Hebrews 2:14)
Both Joshua and Zerubbabel were spoken of as anointed ones who stand before the Lord (Zechariah 4:14).	"Christ" is the New Testament Greek for the Old Testament Hebrew word "Messiah." "Messiah" means "anointed one."

QUESTIONS

God is building his new temple (Romans 12:5). Paul explains the church by comparing it with a "body" (1 Corinthians 12:12–31). God builds this temple by giving gifts to every believer (1 Corinthians 12:7). Some of the gifts the Apostle Paul lists are gifts of wisdom, knowledge, faith, healing, prophecy, tongues, teaching, administration, serving, encouraging, leadership, mercy, and love. Where do you see these gifts in use today?

Prophecies Fulfilled by Jesus

From 400 to 1,500 years before Jesus, Hebrew prophets foretold about the coming Messiah. Jesus fulfilled their prophecies, demonstrating that he was indeed the long-awaited Savior.

Prophecy	Old Testament References	New Testament Fulfillment
Be of the offspring of the woman, shall bruise the serpent's head	**Genesis 3:14, 15** So the LORD God said to the serpent . . . "And I will put enmity between you and the woman, and between your offspring and hers; he will crush your head, and you will strike his heel."	**Galatians 4:4** But when the time had fully come, God sent his Son, born of a woman, born under law, **Hebrews 2:14** Since the children have flesh and blood, he too shared in their humanity so that by his death he might destroy him who holds the power of death . . . that is, the devil. **1 John 3:8** He who does what is sinful is of the devil, because the devil has been sinning from the beginning. The reason the Son of God appeared was to destroy the devil's work.
Be born in the town of Bethlehem of Judea (Judah)	**Micah 5:2-5** "But you, Bethlehem Ephratah, though you are small among the clans of Judah, out of you will come for me one who will be ruler over Israel, whose origins are from of old, from ancient times." . . .	**Matthew 2:1-6** After Jesus was born in Bethlehem in Judea, during the time of King Herod, Magi from the east came to Jerusalem and asked, "Where is the one who has been born king of the Jews? . . ."
Be born a king of the line of David	**Isaiah 9:7** . . . He will reign on David's throne and over his kingdom . . . Also 2 Samuel 7:12, 13; Jeremiah 23:5; 30:9	**Matthew 1:1** A record of the genealogy of Jesus Christ the son of David, the son of Abraham . . . Also Luke 1:32; Acts 13:22, 23
A child to be born	**Isaiah 9:6** For to us a child is born . . . he will be called Wonderful Counselor, Mighty God . . .	**Luke 2:11** Today in the town of David a Saviour has been born to you; he is Christ the Lord.
Be born of a virgin	**Isaiah 7:13, 14** Then Isaiah said, "Hear now, you house of David! Is it not enough to try the patience of men? Will you try the patience of my God also? Therefore the Lord himself will give you a sign: The virgin will be with child and will give birth to a son, and will call him Immanuel (God with us)."	**Matthew 1:18-23** . . . His mother Mary was pledged to be married to Joseph, but before they came together, she was found to be with child through the Holy Spirit. **Luke 1:26-35** . . . God sent the angel . . . to a virgin pledged to be married to a man named Joseph, a descendant of David. The virgin's name was Mary. . . .

Prophecy	Old Testament References	New Testament Fulfillment
Be rejected by his brethren	**Psalm 69:8** I am a stranger to my brothers, an alien to my own mother's sons . . .	**John 7:3-5** Jesus' brothers said to him, "You ought to leave here . . . so that your disciples may see the miracles you do. . . ." For even his own brothers did not believe in him.
Be rejected as capstone	**Psalm 118:22, 23** The stone the builders rejected has become the capstone; the LORD has done this, and it is marvellous in our eyes.	**Matthew 21:42** Jesus said to them, "Have you never read in the Scriptures: "'The stone the builders rejected has become the capstone . . .
The King comes to Jerusalem riding on a donkey	**Zechariah 9:9** . . . See, your king comes to you, righteous and having salvation, gentle and riding on a donkey, on a colt, the foal of a donkey.	**Mark 11:1-10** . . . When they brought the colt to Jesus and threw their cloaks over it, he sat on it. . . . Also Matthew 21:1-5; Luke 19:28-38; John 12:14, 15
Upon his coming, the deaf hear, the blind see	**Isaiah 29:18** In that day the deaf will hear the words of the scroll, and out of gloom and darkness the eyes of the blind will see. **Isaiah 35:5** Then will the eyes of the blind be opened and the ears of the deaf unstopped.	**Matthew 11:5** The blind receive sight, the lame walk, those who have leprosy are cured, the deaf hear, the dead are raised, and the good news is preached to the poor. Also John 9:39; Luke 7:19-22; Mark 7:37
Fulfill promises to Jews, be a light to the Gentiles	**Isaiah 42:6** ". . . I will keep you and will make you to be a covenant for the people and a light for the Gentiles . . ." **Isaiah 49:6** ". . . I will also make you a light for the Gentiles, that you may bring my salvation to the ends of the earth."	**Luke 2:25-32** ". . . a light for revelation to the Gentiles and for glory to your people Israel." **Acts 26:23** ". . . that the Christ would suffer and, as the first to rise from the dead, would proclaim light to his own people and to the Gentiles."
A new everlasting covenant	**Jeremiah 31:31-34** ". . . I will make a new covenant with the house of Israel and with the house of Judah. It will not be like the covenant I made with their forefathers . . . I will put my law in their minds and write it on their hearts. . . ." Also Jeremiah 32:37-40; 50:5	**Luke 22:15-20** . . . "This cup is the new covenant in my blood . . ." **Hebrews 10:15-20** . . . "This is the covenant I will make with them after that time . . ." a new and living way opened for us . . . Also Matthew 26:27-29; Mark 14:22-24; Luke 22:15-20; 1 Corinthians 11:25; Hebrews 8:8-12
Be a priest after the order of Melchizedek	Psalm 110:4	Hebrews 5:1-6; 6:20; 7:15-17

Prophecy	Old Testament References	New Testament Fulfillment
The government is on his shoulders	Isaiah 9:6	Matthew 28:18; 1 Corinthians 15:24, 25
Be a Shepherd who tends his sheep	Isaiah 40:10, 11	John 10:11; Hebrews 13:20; 1 Peter 2:25
The Redeemer to come out of Zion	Isaiah 59:16-20	Romans 11:26, 27
Be Passover sacrifice with no bone broken	**Exodus 12:46** It must be eaten inside one house; take none of the meat outside the house. Do not break any of the bones. **Numbers 9:12** They must not leave any of it till morning or break any of its bones. When they celebrate the Passover, they must follow all the regulations. Also Psalm 34:20	**John 19:31-36** ... But when they came to Jesus and found that he was already dead, they did not break his legs.... These things happened so that the scripture would be fulfilled: "Not one of his bones will be broken."
Be hung upon a tree as a curse for us	**Deuteronomy 21:23** ... Be sure to bury him that same day, because anyone who is hung on a tree is under God's curse. You must not desecrate the land the LORD your God is giving you as an inheritance.	**Galatians 3:13** Christ redeemed us from the curse of the law by becoming a curse for us, for it is written: "Cursed is everyone who is hung on a tree."
Be beaten and spat upon	**Isaiah 50:6** I offered my back to those who beat me, my cheeks to those who pulled out my beard; I did not hide my face from mocking and spitting.	**Matthew 26:67** Then they spat in his face and struck him with their fists. Others slapped him. **Matthew 27:26-30** ... They spat on him, and took the staff and struck him on the head again and again. Also Mark 14:65; 15:15-19; Luke 22:63-65; John 19:1
Be accused and afflicted, but did not open his mouth	**Isaiah 53:7** He was oppressed and afflicted, yet he did not open his mouth; he was led like a lamb to the slaughter, and as a sheep before her shearers is silent, so he did not open his mouth.	**Matthew 27:12** When he was accused by the chief priests and the elders, he gave no answer. **Luke 23:9** He plied him with many questions, but Jesus gave him no answer. Also Matthew 26:62, 63; 27:14; Mark 14:61; 15:5; John 19:9
Be numbered (crucified) with transgressors	**Isaiah 53:12** ... he poured out his life unto death, and was numbered with the transgressors ...	**Matthew 27:38** Two robbers were crucified with him, ... Also Mark 15:27, 28; Luke 22:37; 23:32, 33

Christ
in the Passover

History and Symbolism
of the Passover

Seder and the Lord's Supper Comparison

"For Christ, our Passover lamb, has been sacrificed. Therefore, let us keep the Festival."
—1 Corinthians 5:7-8

OLD TESTAMENT ORIGIN OF THE PASSOVER

THE PASSOVER is the Old Testament feast that celebrates and remembers God's liberation of Israel from Egypt. After Joseph saved Egypt from starvation (Genesis 41), the Israelites lived in Egypt as guests. Eventually, the Egyptians forgot about Joseph and enslaved the Israelites for hundreds of years (Exodus 1:6–14). Overburdened with work and mistreatment, the Israelites suffered a great deal and called out to the Lord. God responded to their cry and raised a great leader, Moses, who challenged the Pharaoh and Egypt's power.

The book of Exodus explains how God freed his people from Egypt. Because of the hardness of Pharaoh's heart, God punished Egypt with ten plagues (Exodus 7–11). However, instead of recognizing the true God of heaven and earth, Pharaoh grew angrier and oppressed the Israelites even more. One way Pharaoh increased the Israelites' suffering was by refusing to give them straw, one of the key materials to produce bricks.

However, God would not be denied. As the plagues continued, the suffering shifted from the Israelites to the Egyptians. The nation paid dearly for Pharaoh's stubbornness. During the last plague, God killed all the first-borns— humans and animals—in the land of Egypt.

God gave his people a way to escape the destruction: the blood of a perfect lamb could take the place of the first-born in the family. God gave Moses specific instructions to follow the night that God's punishment passed over the Israelite homes (Exodus 12). They were to sacrifice a perfect lamb (and mark their door frames), make unleavened bread, and gather bitter herbs. The Israelites ate this meal standing up, ready to leave Egypt at any moment. This celebration is now called the Passover because God "passed over" the homes marked with the lamb's blood. The Passover feast was to be repeated throughout the generations as a memorial forever.

The following information looks at:

- ➤ The Old Testament origin and celebration of the Passover
- ➤ Passover symbolism and how it anticipated Jesus' work
- ➤ The Passover feast's relevance for Christ's followers today
- ➤ A comparison of Jesus with the Passover lamb

THE PASSOVER IN THE BIBLE

In Exodus 12, God gives Moses the instructions
and requirements for the Passover.

EXODUS 12	CHRIST
12:1–2—The feast marked a new year, a new beginning for the Israelites.	In Christ, every believer is a new creation (2 Corinthians 5:17). Old things and the old life are past.
12:5—A male lamb in its first year was taken into the home on the tenth of Nisan (the first month of the Jewish calendar). While in the home, it was closely inspected to see if there were any blemishes or disfigurements. If it was without defect, it was then sacrificed on the fourteenth of Nisan.	Christ was closely inspected by: • Pilate (Matthew 27:11–26; Luke 23:1–6; 13–25; John 18:28–19:16) • Herod (Luke 23:8–12) • Annas (John 18:12–13; 19–24) • Caiaphas (Matthew 26:57). They could find no fault in him. Christ is the "lamb without blemish or defect" (1 Peter 1:19).
12:6—The "whole community" of God's people was required to participate in the sacrifice.	Accepting Christ's sacrifice is required for all who want to be part of God's community (Romans 3:21–26).
12:7, 12, 22—The blood of the sacrificed lamb was applied to the doorframe—the lintel and side posts. Because of the covering of blood, the house was spared from God's plague.	Christ shed his blood to rescue his people. We need to be covered or justified by the blood of the Lamb to be rescued from condemnation (Romans 3:25; 5:9). Christ is the Lamb that takes away the sins of the world (John 1:29).
12:14—The Passover was to be kept as a remembrance forever.	During the Last Supper, Jesus refers to the bread as "my body given for you; do this in remembrance of me" (Luke 22:19).
12:46—God commanded Israel not to break any bones of the sacrificed lamb.	To speed up Jesus' death, the Roman soldiers were going to break his legs. However, Jesus was already dead, so his bones remained unbroken (John 19:32–33).

THE PASSOVER CELEBRATION AND ITS SYMBOLISM

FIRST CUP AND KIDDUSH ("SANCTIFICATION")

SEDER Before the *Seder* began, traditionally a woman lit special candles to mark the commencement of this sacred time. Immediately after this, the head of the table raised the first cup of wine—the cup of sanctification—and blessed it.

LORD'S SUPPER According to Luke 22:17–18, "After taking the cup, he gave thanks and said, 'Take this and divide it among you. For I tell you I will not drink again of the fruit of the vine until the kingdom of God comes.'"

THE FIRST WASHING OF THE HANDS AND THE BITTER HERBS

SEDER As everyone got ready to partake of the Passover meal, the leader of the Passover washed his hands. Then a plate with salted water was passed around into which everyone dipped a piece of lettuce or parsley (*karpas*). The salt was a reminder of the tears the Israelites shed during their bondage in Egypt. The green herb was a reminder of a new beginning.

LORD'S SUPPER Jesus went further than the traditional hand washing and taught his disciples humility by washing their feet (John 13:1–17). During the remembrance of the Israelites' tears, Judas's betrayal was likely also a bitter experience for Jesus (Mark 14:20).

THE AFIKOMEN

SEDER The leader took three *matzo* breads and placed them in a special bag with three compartments. The middle *matzah* was broken and one piece placed back in the *matzo* bag. The other piece was hidden under a pillow and was called *Afikomen*.

LORD'S SUPPER Although the practice of the *Afikomen* goes back to antiquity, it is quite possible that it originated after the Romans destroyed the Second Temple in AD 70. In other words, it probably was not practiced in Jesus' time.

THE AFIKOMEN

✡ A practice in the contemporary celebration of the Passover—possibly also an ancient practice—is to take three *matzo* breads and place them in a special bag with three compartments.

✡ At one point in the celebration, the middle bread is taken out and broken into two pieces. One of the pieces is returned to the middle bag and the other one is hidden under a pillow. Traditionally, children look for it.

✡ When a child finds the piece of *matzah*, the leader of the celebration must "rescue" it by paying some money to the child.

✡ At the end of the meal, when the Passover Seder is complete, the *Afikomen* is revealed.

MESSIANIC SYMBOLISM

✡ We come as children to the Lord and we are rewarded when we find him.

✡ Jewish Christians who continue celebrating the Passover in the traditional way understand this practice to symbolize important Christian beliefs.

✡ The three *matzo* breads placed in the one bag point to God's very nature: Three persons in one.

✡ The breaking of the second bread and hiding it under a pillow symbolize Jesus' sacrifice on the cross and his resurrection from the tomb.

✡ The hiding of the *Afikomen* for the duration of the Seder represents Christ being hidden from our view for three days in the tomb.

✡ Today the *matzo* breads are pierced and striped because of the way the bread is made. In the past, *matzah* looked like pita bread.

✡ Today many Jewish Christians understand the piercing and the stripes to symbolize the piercing of Jesus on the cross (John 19:34) and his flogging by the Roman soldiers (John 19:1).

BASED ON EXODUS 6:6—7, Jewish tradition has incorporated four cups of wine into the Passover celebration. "Therefore, say to the Israelites: 'I am the LORD, and I will bring you out from under the yoke of the Egyptians. I will free you from being slaves to them, and I will redeem you with an outstretched arm and with mighty acts of judgment. I will take you as my own people...'"

The Cup of SANCTIFICATION	"... I will *bring* you..."
The Cup of PLAGUES	"... I will *free* you..."
The Cup of REDEMPTION	"... I will *redeem* you..."
The Cup of PRAISE (also called Cup of Acceptance)	"... I will *take* you..."

THE SECOND CUP AND THE HAGGADAH

SEDER The leader took the second cup of wine (the cup of plagues) and blessed it. No one drank from it until the *Haggadah* ("the telling") was finished. At this point a child asked the four questions and the leader of the ceremony would tell the story of God's redemption in the Exodus. Traditionally, the answer had to cover at least three elements of the Passover celebration: (1) The Passover sacrifice, (2) the bitter herbs, and (3) the unleavened bread (*matzo*).

LORD'S SUPPER In the Gospel account of the Lord's Supper, the words, "This is my body…" are Jesus' re-interpretation of the Passover. It is here that the sacrificed lamb and the unleavened bread receive greater meaning: Jesus is the Lamb of God (John 1:29) sacrificed in our place (1 Peter 1:17–21) and he is the Bread of Life that comes down from heaven (John 6: 33-35).

THE HAGGADAH INCLUDES four questions. Today, the *Haggadah* is the central part of the Passover *Seder*.

1. On all nights we may eat either leavened or unleavened bread, but on this night, only unleavened bread. Why is this night different from all other nights?

2. On all other nights, we eat all kinds of herbs, but on this night, we eat bitter herbs. Why is this night different from all other nights?

3. On all other nights, we do not dip our vegetables even one time, but on this night we dip them twice, in salt water and *charoset*. Why is this night different from all other nights?

4. On all other nights, we eat either sitting or reclining, but on this night, we eat only reclining. Why is this night different from all other nights?

FIRST PART OF THE HALLEL AND THE SECOND CUP

SEDER At the end of the *Haggadah*, the leader raised the second cup of wine and invited all to sing the first part of the *Hallel*, which is the recitation of Psalms 113 and 114. Then everyone drank the second cup, the cup of plagues.

LORD'S SUPPER The New Testament does not give a detailed account of Jesus' last actions, but rather focuses on the New Covenant (1 Cor. 11:25) and Jesus' sacrifice about to occur. Although they might have recited the first part of the *Hallel* and taken the second cup, it is not registered in the Scriptures.

SECOND HAND WASHING AND PASSOVER MEAL

SEDER All washed their hands once again. Then the leader took the *matzo* breads and broke them into pieces. The leader dipped the bread into a mixture of bitter herbs and distributed them to the participants. The meal was then taken.

LORD'S SUPPER As was traditional in the celebration of the Passover, Jesus dipped a piece of bread; however, he used this moment to indicate who his betrayer would be (John 13:26).

THE GRACE AFTER MEALS AND THE THIRD CUP

SEDER When the meal was finished, no one ate any other food. Instead, the leader of the celebration poured a third cup of wine. Everyone offered another blessing on the third cup of wine, called the cup of redemption, and drank from this cup.

LORD'S SUPPER After the meal, Jesus got up, took a *matzah* bread, and said, "This is my body given for you; do this in remembrance of me" (Luke 22:19). Then he continued with the third cup. He blessed it and said, "This is the cup of the new covenant in my blood; do this, whenever you drink it, in remembrance of me" (1 Corinthians 11:25).

THE SECOND PART OF THE HALLEL AND THE FOURTH CUP

SEDER Once everyone drank the third cup, they recited the second part of the *Hallel* (praise), which consists of Psalms 115–118. No one drank wine between the third cup and the end of the second part of the *Hallel*. At the end of the singing, they drank the fourth cup of wine, called the cup of praise. Then the *Seder* ended.

LORD'S SUPPER Jesus and the disciples finished the Lord's Supper, and Matthew tells us, "When they had sung a hymn, they went out to the Mount of Olives" (Matthew 26:30). The hymn was probably the *Hallel*. The fourth cup was not drunk! "I tell you, I will not drink of this fruit of the vine from now on until that day when I drink it anew with you in my Father's kingdom" (Matthew 26:29). The last cup of the Passover will be drunk at the wedding feast of the Lamb (Revelation 19:9).

THE LORD'S SUPPER

The Passover was a celebration, remembrance, thanksgiving and participation in God's mighty acts of salvation for his people. The New Testament equivalent of the Passover, the Lord's Supper, functions in similar ways for Christians today.

1. The Lord's Supper is a time of remembrance and thanksgiving (Luke 22:19; 1 Corinthians 11:24–25).

2. The Lord's Supper is a time for refreshing and communion (Romans 5:10; 1 Corinthians 10:16).

3. The Lord's Supper is a time for anticipation and recommitment (1 Corinthians 11:26, 28–29).

PASSOVER TERMS

Afikomen comes from a Greek word meaning "that which comes last." It is a piece of *matzah* hidden during the *Seder*.

Betzah is a boiled and roasted egg used in the Passover meal.

Barekh is the after-meal blessing.

Charoset is a sweet apple mixture.

Haggadah means "the telling." It refers to the book used to explain the *Seder* service.

Hallel is Hebrew for "praise." Psalms 113–118 are used for prayers of praise during the *Seder*.

Karpas is one of the symbolic foods in the *Seder*, usually parsley.

Kiddush is Hebrew for a prayer of sanctification or consecration.

Ma Nishtanah means "what is different?" and represents the four questions of the *Haggadah*.

Maggid is the telling of the story of the Exodus.

Maror is Hebrew for "bitter." Usually horseradish, it is one of the symbolic foods in the *Seder*.

Matzah/Matzo is bread made without leaven. Generally, *matzah* is bread (singular) and *matzo* is the meal itself or breads (plural).

Nirtzah is the conclusion of the *Seder*.

Pesach is Hebrew for "Passover."

Seder means "set order," the procedure or agenda for the celebration of the *Pesach*.

Shulhan Orekh is the eating of the *Seder* meal.

Tzafun is the eating of the *Afikomen*.

Urkhatz is the washing of the hands.

Yahatz is the breaking of the *matzo*.

Principal Author: Benjamin Galan, MTS, ThM, Adjunct Professor of OT Hebrew and Literature at Fuller Seminary.
Consultant: Rev. Barry Goldman

Rose bible basics:

Jesus

STUDY GUIDE

A FREE downloadable version of this study guide is available at rose-publishing.com. Click on "News & Info," then on "Downloads."

The **leader guide** covers each chapter of this book and includes teaching tips and additional resources.
The **study guide** includes discussion questions and worksheets.

What participants will gain from this study:
- Understand basic beliefs about who Jesus is and the importance of his death and resurrection.
- Be encouraged to grow closer to Jesus through learning about his names, words, and deeds.
- Learn how to apply Jesus' teachings in daily life.

LEADER GUIDE

Spend time in prayer before each study session and pray for each participant.

In the first session, ask participants to introduce themselves to the group and share what they hope to gain from the study or why they joined this study. Introduce participants to the purposes of this study.

CHAPTER 1: WHO IS JESUS?
Main Idea
Jesus is the Christ and the Son of God. He came to save the world and made that salvation possible through his death and resurrection.

Teaching Tips
Open this session by having participants brainstorm all the words they think of when they hear the name Jesus. Write all the words on a whiteboard or easel pad. Identify which themes you see emerging. Explain that as Christians we are to become like Jesus, so how we view him affects how we live our lives.

Digging Deeper
Check out the Apostle's Creed, one of the earliest statements of faith Christian leaders used to clarify basic Christian beliefs—especially about Jesus. See www.ccel.org/creeds/apostles.creed.html

Worksheet Key
(1) False (2) e (3) d (4) False (5) c

CHAPTER 2: JESUS: FACT & FICTION
Main Idea
The New Testament accurately tells us about Jesus' life, ministry, death and resurrection.

Teaching Tips
You many not have enough time to cover all the controversial topics in this chapter, so encourage participants to pick a few topics that most interest them, and spend the majority of the class time focusing on those topics.

Digging Deeper
For a video segment to show during this session check out the DVD *The Real Jesus: A Defense of the Historicity & Divinity of Christ* (The Apologetics Group: 2008).

For more on specific topics mentioned in this chapter see *Gospels: "Lost" & Found* (Discusses the Gnostic gospels); *Pop Spirituality & the Truth* (Covers Eckhart Tolle, Deepak Chopra, The Secret); *50 Proofs for the New Testament* (Archeological finds). Available at www.rose-publishing.com

Worksheet Key
(1) d (2) False (3) d (4) False (5) a

CHAPTER 3: GOSPELS SIDE BY SIDE

Main Idea

The four Gospels have four human authors, but only one divine Author. Their four points of view arrive at one conclusion: Jesus is not a mere man; he is the Son of God.

Teaching Tips

Make a transparency or laminated page of the map "Israel During Jesus' Time." Using a wet-erase marker track Jesus' travels to show how often Jesus traveled and in which areas he preached and performed miracles.

Digging Deeper

For a complete harmony see *A Harmony of the Gospels (NAS)* (Harper One: 1986) or *The NIV Harmony of the Gospels* (HarperCollins: 1988) both by Robert L. Thomas and Stanley Gundry.

Worksheet Key

(1) c (2) d (3) True (4) False (5) three

CHAPTER 4: THE BEATITUDES

Main Idea

The Beatitudes are about life in the kingdom of God—a life that Jesus teaches is far better than the way of the world.

Teaching Tips

Discussion questions are located within the chapter pages. Because some of the questions are more personal than others, be sure to select questions appropriate for the level of sharing that participants are comfortable with.

Digging Deeper

Put the Beatitudes in context in the Sermon on the Mount. For an outline and explanation of the Sermon on the Mount, see Bible commentaries such as *World Biblical Commentary: Matthew 1–13* by Donald A. Hagner (Thomas Nelson Publishers: 1993).

Worksheet Key

(1) b (2) False (3) b (4) True (5) c

CHAPTER 5: THE LORD'S PRAYER

Main Idea

God is our holy and loving Father who cares for our needs and the needs of others.

Teaching Tips

This is a chapter on prayer, so leave plenty of time for group prayer. Pray together by following the seven attributes of God in the seven parts of the Lord's Prayer.

Sing or recite together the Lord's Prayer to open and/or close the session.

Digging Deeper

For more on prayer see *Alone with God* by John MacArthur, Jr. (Cook Communications Ministries: 1995). The "How Can I Pray?" section in this chapter is an excerpt from *Alone with God*.

Worksheet Key

(1) False (2) d (3) False (4) e (5) e

CHAPTER 6: NAMES OF JESUS

Main Idea

The names of Jesus reveal who he is and how he relates to us.

Teaching Tips

Choose as many names of Jesus as time permits and use the names in prayer, emphasizing their meaning and relevance in our lives. (For example, pray: "Lord Jesus, our Bread of Life, you sustain our lives by...")

Digging Deeper

Compare and contrast the names of Jesus with the names of God and the Holy Spirit. For a listing, see *Names of God* and *Names of the Holy Spirit* pamphlets. Available at www.rose-publishing.com

Worksheet Key

(1) True (2) b (3) d (4) a (5) True

CHAPTER 7: CHRIST IN THE OLD TESTAMENT

Main Idea

Christ is the key to what God has been pointing to in all the history of God's people.

Teaching Tips

Discussion questions are located within the chapter pages.

Encourage participants to pick a few that are most persuasive to them. Choose a handful of prophecies and types to discuss more in depth.

Bring commentaries, Bible dictionaries, and Bible handbooks to the session to help participants go in depth on a few of these prophecies and types.

Digging Deeper

To prepare for teaching this class read more about Messianic prophecies in *The Messiah in the Old Testament* by W.C. Kaiser, Jr., (Grand Rapids: Zondervan, 1995).

Worksheet Key

(1) Joseph (2) Melchizedek (3) Noah (4) Samuel (5) Joshua (6) Adam (7) David (8) Abraham (9) Elijah (10) Moses

CHAPTER 8: CHRIST IN THE PASSOVER

Main Idea

Jesus Christ is the perfect Lamb who takes away the sin of the world. We remember this every time we partake of the Lord's Supper.

Teaching Tips

Begin the session by reading the Passover in Exodus 12:1–14 and Jesus' Last Supper in Matthew 26:17–30.

Digging Deeper

Do more than just teach about the Seder—experience a Christian Seder together. See *Christ in the Passover* pamphlet and/or PowerPoint® presentation for a how-to guide in observing a Passover celebration for Christians. Available at www.rose-publishing.com.

Worksheet Key

(1) d (2) b (3) True (4) False (5) Redemption

Feedback

To improve future studies, be sure to get feedback from the group about teaching style, meeting location, discussion time, material covered, length of study, and group size. Choose a method that best suits your group: Anonymous evaluation sheet, e-mail response or questionnaire, open discussion. See the questions at the end of this study guide.

Note: The inclusion of a work or website does not necessarily mean endorsement of all its contents or of other works by the same author(s).

STUDY GUIDE

The study guide which begins on the following page includes discussion questions and a worksheet for each chapter.

WHO IS JESUS?

Worksheet

1. True or False? Jesus was human while on earth and became divine after his resurrection.

2. Which is part of Jesus' message?
   a. Repentance
   b. Belief
   c. Himself
   d. (a) and (b)
   e. All of the above

3. Jesus referred to himself in the Gospels as:
   a. The gate
   b. The bread
   c. The book
   d. (a) and (b)
   e. All of the above

4. True or False? Jesus' betrayal and execution came as a surprise to Jesus.

5. Which of the following is true of Jesus' second coming?
   a. Jesus did not speak of it while on earth
   b. Only believers will see him when he returns
   c. Only believers will rule with him
   d. (b) and (c)

Discussion Questions

1. Books and movies portray Jesus as various types: Jesus the revolutionary, Jesus the martyr, Jesus the rabbi, Jesus meek and mild, Jesus the healer, etc. How do you view Jesus when you read his story in the Gospels?
2. When Jesus preached that the "kingdom of God is near" (Mark 1:15), what might his first-century Jewish audience have understood it to mean? What do you think people today understand it to mean?
3. What does it mean that Jesus was the Christ, the Messiah? How do people nowadays understand these terms?
4. Look at the *Beliefs about Jesus* chart. Are some of the beliefs more difficult than others for you to accept? Which ones and why?
5. In what ways did Jesus' resurrection change the lives of his disciples? How does it change the lives of believers today?

JESUS: FACT & FICTION

Worksheet

1. What are the "Gnostic Gospels"?
   a. Gospels based on the book of Matthew
   b. Writings that portray more accurately who Jesus was
   c. Writings that include eyewitness testimony about Jesus
   d. Writings produced in the second and third centuries AD

2. True or False? The first-century historian Josephus does not mention Jesus in his writings.

3. Of the following which is not true about the Buddhist manuscript claimed to be discovered in the 18th century.
   a. The manuscript was claimed to be discovered in a Buddhist monastery.
   b. Notovitch claimed the manuscript described how Jesus traveled around India.
   c. The manuscript that Notovitch claimed was discovered in India was actually discovered in Egypt.
   d. No manuscript has been produced to verify Notovich's claims that it even exists.

4. True or False? All rabbis in Jesus' time were required to be married.

5. Which is true about the "Jesus Family Tomb"?
   a. Joseph and Jesus were common names in the first century.
   b. Most biblical scholars accept the "Jesus family tomb" theory.
   c. It provides proof that Jesus and Mary Magdalene were married.
   d. (a) and (b)

Discussion Questions

1. When you hear challenges to Jesus' existence or the reliability of the Gospels, how do you usually respond?

2. Why do you think in recent years more and more people are eager to remake Jesus into a New Age practitioner or an Eastern guru?

3. Does it matter that the Gospel accounts of Jesus' life are reliable? Why or why not?

4. Read 1 Corinthians 15:12–18. Why is Jesus' resurrection important for our salvation?

5. What is one topic in this chapter that you would like to learn more about?

GOSPELS SIDE BY SIDE

Worksheet

1. What is not true about the Gospel of Matthew?
   a. Written for a Jewish audience
   b. Presents Jesus as the Messiah King
   c. Symbolically represented as a bull
   d. Possibly written in the Jewish language of his day and translated into Greek

2. What is not true about the Gospel of John?
   a. Written for the whole world
   b. Presents Jesus as the Word of God
   c. Symbolically represented as an eagle
   d. Is one of the Synoptic Gospels

3. True or False? Jesus began his public ministry in Galilee.

4. True or False? Ancient biographers gave much emphasis to keeping the historical sequence accurate.

5. Jesus' public ministry lasted approximately _____ years.

Discussion Questions

1. Of the four Gospels which do you read most often? Why do you think this is so?

2. When you see discrepancies between the Gospel accounts how do you react? Doubt? Further study? Disregard it? Prayer? Faith?

3. How might different points of view from different writers about Jesus' life be a good thing?

4. Name several expectations we have for biographies in the 21st century. Would the Gospels meet those expectations?

5. What are some reasons the Gospel writers may have had for centering so much of their attention on the last week of Jesus' ministry?

THE BEATITUDES

Worksheet

1. The Latin word beatus, from where we get beatitude, means:
   a. Kingdom
   b. Happy
   c. Peace
   d. None of the above

2. True or False? By fulfilling the beatitude commandments a person will be allowed to enter the kingdom of heaven.

3. To be "meek" in the Bible means to be:
   a. Passive
   b. Humble
   c. Shy
   d. Proud

4. True or False? Having a pure heart is not the result of personal effort and not something we work toward.

5. When God makes right (justifies) sinners, this means that they:
   a. Can only do what is right
   b. Are still "legally" guilty of their sin before God
   c. Have Christ's righteousness applied to them
   d. Earned their righteousness through practicing the beatitude

(Discussion questions are located within the chapter.)

THE LORD'S PRAYER

Worksheet

1. True or False? Addressing God as "Father" in prayer was a common practice in Jesus' day.

2. To "hallow" God's name means to:
   a. Misuse God's name
   b. Speak God's name
   c. Clear God's name as justified
   d. Honor God's name as sacred

3. True or False? God's kingdom will come in the future, but is not yet here and now.

4. The "debts" referred to in "forgive us our debts" are:
   a. Our sins
   b. Our spiritual debts
   c. Our neglect of doing good
   d. (a) and (b)
   e. All of the above

5. By asking God for "our daily bread" we are:
   a. Acknowledging that our life depends on his mercy
   b. Not taking God's mercy for granted
   c. Asking for physical things we need
   d. (a) and (b)
   e. All of the above

Discussion Questions

1. When did you first hear the Lord's Prayer? Did you grow up reciting it? Singing it? Is it new to you?

2. How does addressing God as "Father" in prayer change the way you see God, and the way you see yourself in relation to him?

3. The Lord's Prayer shows us that we need to ask God for our daily bread. What are some "daily breads" in your life that you can ask God for on a day-to-day basis?

4. With so many good reasons to forgive, why do you think it is often difficult to forgive? How can you learn to forgive others more?

5. In Matthew 6:14–15 we learn that God will not forgive us if we refuse to forgive others. Is there someone you are holding resentment against?

NAMES OF JESUS

Worksheet

1. True or False? The word Christ is the Greek translation of Messiah which means "anointed one."

2. Which name of Jesus focuses on Jesus as the fulfillment of the sacrificial system and the sacrifice that pays for our sins?
   a. Shiloh
   b. Lamb of God
   c. Emmanuel
   d. All of the above

3. Which name of Jesus focuses on Jesus as the One we rely on?
   a. Bread of Life
   b. True Vine
   c. Chief Cornerstone
   d. All of the above

4. Jesus, the Greek word for Yeshua, means:
   a. Jehovah is salvation
   b. God with us
   c. Witness
   d. Messenger of the Covenant

5. True or False? Jesus is called Apostle in the New Testament?

Discussion Questions

1. There are many names of Jesus in the Bible. How do so many names help us to relate to Jesus better?

2. What are some similarities you notice between the names of God and the names of Jesus?

3. One of Jesus' titles is Son of God and believers are called sons of God. How is our relationship to God similar to Jesus' and in what ways is it different?

4. Which names of Jesus do you find easy to use when praying? Which ones are difficult for you to use?

CHRIST IN THE OLD TESTAMENT

Worksheet

Fill in the blanks using the names in the list below. Use each name only once.

Adam
Noah
Abraham
Melchizedek
Joseph
Moses
Joshua
Samuel
David
Elijah

1. As _____ was unjustly condemned, Christ was unjustly condemned.

2. As _____ blessed Abraham, Christ blesses Abraham's spiritual children.

3. As _____'s ark provided refuge for all kinds of animals, Christ's body (the church) provides salvation for all, both Jew and Gentile.

4. As _____ was given to Israel after a long silence from God, Christ was given after a long silence from God.

5. As _____ parted the Jordan River, Christ walked on water.

6. As _____'s shame required the death of an animal, Christ's was slain to cover our shame.

7. As _____'s experiences are reflected in the Psalms, Christ's experiences are the fulfillment of those psalms.

8. As _____'s son's birth was to be a blessing to all nations, all nations are blessed through Christ.

9. As _____ traveled in the wilderness for 40 days and was cared for by an angel, Christ was in the wilderness for 40 days and angels took care of him.

10. As _____ prayed for Miriam to be healed of leprosy, Christ healed lepers.

(Discussion questions are located within the chapter.)

CHRIST IN THE PASSOVER

Worksheet

1. Which is true about the Passover described in Exodus?
   a. It marks a new year
   b. No bones of the lamb were to be broken
   c. Only the males of the households participated in the meal
   d. (a) and (b)
   e. All of the above

2. The Afikomen is:
   a. The four cups
   b. Broken matzah
   c. Parsley or another bitter herb
   d. The Pesach

3. True or False? Haggadah means "the telling."

4. True or False? Only Jesus drank from the fourth cup (the cup of praise).

5. Fill in the blank: The four cups are Sanctification, Plagues, _____, and Praise.

Discussion Questions

1. Before reading this chapter, how familiar were you with Passover? Have you ever participated in a Seder? If so, what was your experience?

2. What is one thing you learned about Jesus' Last Supper that you didn't know before reading this chapter?

3. Read Romans 3:25–26 and 5:9. The Apostle Paul wrote this in the 1st century. How would you explain these ideas to people in the 21st century in a way they could understand?

FEEDBACK

1. What did you learn through this study that deepened your relationship with God and/or helped you understand biblical teachings better? _____
   _____
   _____

2. What was your favorite thing about this study, and why? _____
   _____
   _____

3. How could the meeting location, setting, length, or time be improved? _____
   _____
   _____

4. Did you think the material covered was too difficult, too easy, or just right? _____
   _____
   _____

5. What would you like to see different about the group discussions? _____
   _____
   _____

6. What would you like to see different about the worksheets? _____
   _____
   _____

7. What topic would you like to learn more about? _____
   _____
   _____

MORE Rose Bible Basics
Bible Reference Made Easy

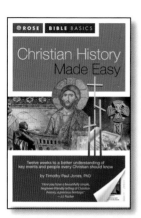

Christian History Made Easy

This easy-to-read book brings to life the most important events and people in Christian history that every believer should know. Author Timothy Paul Jones, Ph.D., makes Christian history refreshingly fun while at the same time informative and engaging. From kings to monks, revivals to revolutions—follow the fascinating history of the Christian faith from the time of Jesus to today.

Easy to use in the classroom, at church, for homeschooling or personal study. Includes study guide.

224 pages, 6 x 9-inch paperback ISBN: 9781596363281

Jesus

This easy-to-understand book provides a biblically centered approach to learning who Jesus is and why his powerful message of salvation matters today. Includes: the Gospels side by side, 50 names of Jesus, the Beatitudes and the Lord's Prayer. Learn how to confront popular myths about Jesus, and to show that he is truly the Messiah (the Christ)—the hope of all people for all time!

Packed with full-color photos, illustrations and charts, as well as numerous Bible verses and references for further study. Perfect for new believers classes, Bible studies, personal study, or as a handy Bible reference. Includes study guide.

128 pages, 6 x 9-inch paperback ISBN: 9781596363243

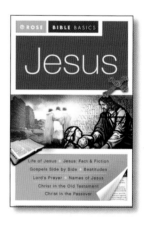

God in Real Life

To navigate life's tough choices, teens and young adults need a real relationship with God in their real life. This full-color book provides clear, biblical answers to their questions about Jesus, Christianity, other religions, pop occultism, evolution, sex, decision making, faith, and growing closer to God.

Great for youth groups, Bible studies, new believers, or anyone who wants to understand what it means to be a follower of Jesus at school, at home, and with friends. Includes study guide.

128 pages, 6 x 9-inch paperback ISBN: 9781596363250

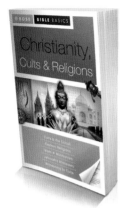

Free, downloadable study guide *at rose-publishing.com.*
Click on "News & Info," then on "Downloads."

Christianity, Cults & Religions

Helps clarify differences between the beliefs and practices of various religions, cults, and new religious movements. Includes topics such as: Who is God? Who is Jesus Christ? What is salvation? What happens after death?

Contains comparisons of biblical Christianity with Anthroposophy, Bahá'í, Buddhism, Christian Science, Eastern mysticism, Hare Krishna, Hinduism, Islam, Jehovah's Witnesses, Judaism, Latter-day Saints/Mormons, Muslims, Nation of Islam, New age movement, Soka Gakkai International, Scientology (Dianetics), Theosophy, TM (Transcendental Meditation), Unification Church, Unity School, Wicca, Kabbalah, and more.

128 pages, 6 x 9-inch paperback
ISBN: 9781596362024

Names of God and Other Bible Studies

Contains favorite Bible studies to use in small groups, church groups, and for individual study. Includes studies on the Names of God, Names of Jesus, Names of the Holy Spirit, Trinity, Ten Commandments, Lord's Prayer, Beatitudes, Fruit of the Spirit, and Armor of God. Includes color charts, illustrations, and photos throughout.

128 pages, 6 x 9-inch paperback.   ISBN: 9781596362031

The Bible at a Glance

This full color book is an introduction to basic Bible knowledge contains a Bible overview summarizing each book of the Bible, a Bible time line comparing Bible history and world history side by side, steps to studying the Bible, Then & Now Bible maps, where to find favorite Bible verses, Bible promises, the basics of the Christian life, and a Bible translations comparison chart.

128 pages, 6 x 9-inch paperback.   ISBN: 9781596362000

Being Jesus' Disciple

This book covers the basics of discipleship in one easy-to-read book — with a number of full-color diagrams and charts to help people grasp how to be Jesus' disciple in today's world.

Chapters cover the topics that every Christian must learn to grow and mature in their faith:

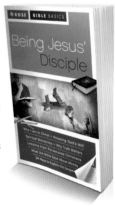

- Who I Am in Christ —30 ways that Christ has changed me.
- Knowing God's Will — 3 ways to make sure you are going in the right direction, 9 reasons you can trust God to make the best decisions for your life, 8 reminders to help you conquer fear.
- Explaining the Gospel — Here are 24 ways to explain the Good News about Jesus Christ, as well as 4 popular "salvation illustrations".
- Why Truth Matters — Know what you believe and why about God, Jesus, and salvation.
- And much more

128 pages, 6 x 9-inch paperback.   ISBN: 9781596364158

MORE Rose Bible REFERENCE
Bible Reference Made Easy

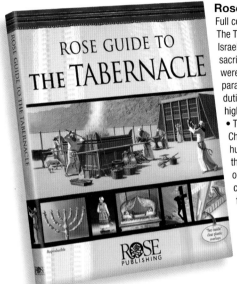

Rose Guide to the Tabernacle
Full color with clear overlays and reproducible pages
The Tabernacle ("tent of meeting") was the place where the Israelites worshiped God after the Exodus. Learn how the sacrifices, utensils, and even the structure of the tabernacle were designed to show us something about God. See the parallels between the Old Testament sacrifices and priests' duties, and Jesus' service as the perfect sacrifice and perfect high priest. See how:
• The Tabernacle was built • The sacrifices pointed Jesus Christ • The design of the tent revealed God's holiness and humanity's need for God • The Ark of the Covenant was at the center of worship. Clear plastic overlays show inside/outside of the tabernacle; plus dozens of reproducible charts. You may reproduce up to 300 copies of any chart free of charge for your classroom. 128 pages.

Finalist in the Christian Book Award

Deluxe "Then and Now" Bible Maps
Book with CD-ROM!
See where Bible places are today with "Then and Now" Bible maps with clear plastic overlays of modern cities and countries. This deluxe edition comes with a CD-ROM that gives you a JPG of each map to use in your own Bible material as well as PDFs of each map and overlay to create your own handouts or overhead transparencies. PowerPoint fans can create their own presentations with these digitized maps.

Hardcover. ISBN-13: 9781596361638

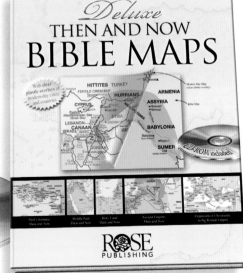

INCLUDES DISK

Other Rose Publishing Books

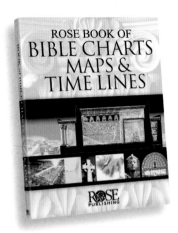

Rose Book of Bible Charts, Maps & Time Lines

Dozens of popular Rose Publishing Bible charts, maps, and time lines in one spiral-bound book. Reproduce up to 300 copies of any chart free of charge.

- Christianity, Cults & Religions
- Denominations Comparison
- Christian History Time Line
- How We Got the Bible
- Tabernacle
- Temple and High Priest
- Islam and Christianity

- Jesus' Genealogy
- Bible Time Line
- Bible Bookcase
- Bible Overview
- Ark of the Covenant
- Bible maps
- Trinity, and more.

192 pages. Hardcover.   ISBN-13: 9781596360228

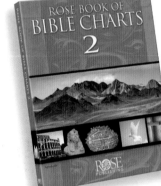

Rose Book of Bible Charts 2

Here are dozens of popular Rose charts in one book! Topics include • Bible Translations comparison chart • Why Trust the Bible? • Heroes of the Old Testament • Women of the Bible • Life of Paul • Christ in the Old Testament • Christ in the Passover • Names of Jesus • Beatitudes • Lord's Prayer • Where to Find Favorite Bible Verses • Christianity and Eastern Religions • Worldviews Comparison • 10 Q & A on Mormonism/Jehovah's Witnesses/Magic/Atheism and many others! Hardcover with a spine covering a spiral binding. 240 pages ISBN: 9781596362758

Rose Book of Bible & Christian History Time Lines

Six thousand years and 20 feet of time lines in one hard-bound cover! This unique resource allows you to easily store and reference two time lines in book form. These gorgeous time lines printed on heavy chart paper, can also be slipped out of their binding and posted in a hallway or large room for full effect.
• The 10-foot Bible Time Line compares Scriptural events with world history and Middle East history. Shows hundreds of facts; includes dates of kings, prophets, battles, and key events.
• The 10-foot Christian History Time Line begins with the life of Jesus and continues to the present day. Includes key people and events that all Christians should know. Emphasis on world missions, the expansion of Christianity, and Bible translation in other languages. These two time lines are connected end-to-end to form one long teaching aid.
Hardcover. ISBN-13: 9781596360846